Evolve

From Heart Breaks to Hearts Healed

A compilation of stories inspired by the First Wives Club

VISIONARY AUTHOR

PATRICE WEBB BUSH

Published by Victorious You Press ™

Copyright © 2020 By Patrice Webb Bush

All rights reserved.

No part of this book may be reproduced, distributed or transmitted in any form by any means, graphic, electronic, or mechanical, including photocopy, recording, taping, or by any information storage or retrieval system, without permission in writing from the author except in the case of reprints in the context of reviews, quotes, or references.

Unless otherwise indicated, scripture quotations are from the Holy Bible, New King James Version. All rights reserved.

Printed in the United States of America

ISBN: 978-1-7340609-9-7

For details email vyp.joantrandall@gmail.com
or visit us at www.victoriousyoupress.com

Dedication

This book is dedicated to the incredibly strong, brave, and beautiful ladies of the First Wives Club (FWC). The FWC is a safe place for wives to come together and take off their capes and erase the "S" on their chest. FWC is where women can lay down the role of wife, mommy, career woman, and every other role we play and just be WOMAN. Ladies, I thank you for embracing, owning, and your dedication to our "safe place." This book is an extension of your voice…of the voice that is so strong, yet weak, so brave, yet scared, loud yet humble, and sometimes aggressive yet submissive. I love your strength and admire your power within. Thank you for riding this journey with me. #FWCStrong #Sisterhood

CONTENTS

INTRODUCTION 1

FORGIVENESS AFTER BETRAYAL: *April Taylor* 5

DISCOVERING THE GIFTS OF ME: *Janet L. Jacobs* 19

NOTHING BUT A MIRACLE: *Shania Elliott-Mcdowell* 37

MY 9-1-1 MOMENT: *Michelle W. Pennington* 49

THE GAME CHANGER: *Michele Magaña* 63

THE MILITARY DID NOT BREAK US: *Monica Busanet* 79

THEY SAVED ME: *Shumon Spears Hudson* 95

LOVING AN ADDICT: *Deleisha L. Webb* 113

RESOURCES 131

ABOUT THE AUTHORS 133

INTRODUCTION

Wife, mother of three daughters, successful business owner, award-winning author, influencer and dynamic keynote speaker; a trailblazer in business and stewardship, the recipient of a multitude of academic accomplishments and helped to restore over hundreds of marriages. Sounds like a PROFOUND woman right? What if I told you that same woman is on the brink of divorce, feels drained, has failed more times than she can count, struggles with insecurities, cried herself to sleep for an entire year, thought about closing her business at the height of its success, almost lost herself trying to become someone she was not and sometimes felt like a bad mom? Would you view her differently? Would you judge her? Would it change her value as a woman, as a human being? Would you call her a hypocrite?

Well that woman is me, Patrice Bush, the owner and relationship therapist of It Takes 2 Marriage Coaching. My private practice is one of the most successful marriage counseling practices in North Carolina. I have served over 850 couples through pre-marital counseling, marital counseling, destination marriage retreats, healing retreats and many other relationship events across 34 states. My accomplishments don't keep me from being human. My failures, struggles, hang ups AND my explosive success are what has molded me into this woman…a woman who is evolving from heart-break to a heart-healed.

Five years ago, while hosting a Valentine marriage retreat, I found myself pinned in a corner by six wives. I was bombarded with, "Patrice, I need some time with you alone. Are the women going to be able to talk to you by ourselves? Girl, there is something I need to tell you that I don't want to share in front of my husband. He doesn't always understand my heart and I am not sure how to tell him how I feel! Sometimes I just want to scream because I have lost myself between being a wife, mom and career woman. I love my kids but I need a break from being a mom sometime." I remember thinking, "Wow, these women really need their own safe haven, their own space to call their own. A space where they can grow, change and evolve into stronger, better women, moms who don't beat themselves up and wives who adorn their husbands while being loved with reciprocation."

Three years ago, God gave me the answer to those wives' questions. He told me to begin the First Wives Club. The First Wives Club is not for first time wives, but for any wife who wears an "S" on her chest and a cape on her back. These wives need the opportunity to erase the S, get her cape washed, put her feet up and just be a woman. This book is just that, it's an opportunity for YOU to take off your "S", snuggle up in a corner and just be a woman. You will take the journey with eight women, some who have struggled to conceive children, others who survived domestic violence or healed from infidelity. These are women who married addicts, overcame social justice or who served our country but failed to serve their marriage.

Keep your tissues close by but make sure your belly is ready for laughter too because this journey will take you through every emotion with these uniquely evolving women who went through hell but lived to tell the story. These stories are raw and uncut, yet authentic and genuine. Make sure you make note of the resources in the back, as they exist to help you in case you find yourself in "hell" and need help finding a way out.

Oh….what about me? Is my story in this book? The short answer is no. I am the visionary author for this book because this is my form of activism. This book is my way to introduce the world to the multifaceted woman, the woman who is both strong and weak, both submissive and assertive, educated yet makes mistakes, is hurting and healed; evolved YET still evolving. I produced this book for every woman who can relate to these stories, every woman who cries in the bathroom mirror, then puts her make up on and shows up like nothing is wrong. I am your advocate, your backbone, your megaphone, your cheerleader because YOU are ME. My story is next, but your story is now. Stay tuned for my evolution story, but for now let's takes this journey together. Buckle up…it's going to be a bumpy ride.

FORGIVENESS AFTER BETRAYAL

By: April Taylor

Growing up every young girl has a dream of getting married to the man of her dreams, having kids and living happily ever after. At the age of seventeen I met the love of my life and I was married by twenty-one. Little did I know that my life would take a turn just a few years into our marriage and I was not prepared for the things we would soon experience. Tim and I had a long-distance relationship for about 4 years, he is from Delaware and I'm from South Carolina. We met through church. Years passed and we would visit each other as often as we could. We would even write each other letters. Tim proposed on September, 2010 and by

November 18 we were married. We had dreamed of this day and finally we were together with our son and our journey would begin.

Fast forward to four years into our marriage, I was sitting on my bed seven months pregnant with our third child, when I received a phone call. The person on the other line said, "I'm not sure what is going on but check your social media." At that point I became confused and I simply said "ok." To my surprise, on social media I saw a screenshot posted of my husband having an inappropriate conversation with another lady. At that moment, my heart beat faster and my hands grew sweaty. I hollered for my husband.

I looked at him and I said, "Explain this?" With a dumb look on his face he says, "Oh it's nothing like that, just a conversation. I swear it's nothing." That wasn't good enough for me. I wanted answers, so I reached out to the lady and she assured me it was nothing at all. At that point, I didn't believe a word he was saying but he reassured me nothing was going on.

This was the first red flag, but I ignored it and trusted his word and we continued to move forward in our marriage. In the back of my mind I'm like, this can't be happening to me. Tim knew how I had been hurt in my previous relationship. He promised me he wouldn't put me through that again. We were able to move forward by being brutally honest with one another. Tim's behavior changed. I forgave him, well at least I thought I did because after all, it was just a conversation. From that point on we were on a good stretch. He was working on himself to become a better husband and I was working to become a better wife. A few months later our daughter was born, and it was the happiest day of our lives. Our marriage couldn't get any better. Some time went by and my husband got a new job, and I took on the responsibility of taking care of a sick loved one. I was so overwhelmed taking care of that sick family member and our kids that I didn't realize I was neglecting my husband. Tim would always say, "You're taking on too much. I want to spend time with my wife but you're always busy." My typical response would be, "I hear you and I promise I'm going to do better." I'll never forget I had a relative tell me "baby you're young you should be enjoying life; you got a husband and kids. You got too much on your plate caring for this sick loved one and it's going to cost you your marriage if you don't slow down and focus on your family." By the time I realized what was going on, my husband was slowly pulling away and never wanted to be home.

Here I am 26 years old and on the verge of a mental breakdown because I had so much on my plate and I didn't know when to say "no." At this point, everything became an argument between Tim and I. We were at each other's throats every day and I couldn't take it anymore. I became so overwhelmed; I gave up the responsibility of caring for the family member. I had tried so hard to please everyone, but enough was enough for putting everyone's needs before mine. So I refocused on my husband and children, by that time it was too late. My husband had started to look elsewhere. In hindsight I was too exhausted to notice the signs.

The day I found out was the day all hell broke loose. Without the distraction of the sick family member, I began to notice that my husband was at work all the time. I kept thinking, "Nobody loves their job that much!" When he *was* home, he was glued to his phone, watching sports or isolated in the bedroom. All these were red flags that I had missed. Where was the husband I had married? I didn't recognize this person so I had begun to ask, "Hey are you alright? Is there anything we need to discuss, anything you want to tell me?"

His answer would always be, "No I'm good." He would avoid any kind of conversation with me. His responses were consistently short and simple. Even though I was absolutely certain he was cheating, I had no proof. So I gave him every opportunity to just be honest with me and he still would not come clean. He never admitted to cheating, which led me to go searching for evidence. I never found anything, and he would say you're crazy, you're just imagining things. It became so bad we would have arguments over the craziest things which gave him a reason to blow up and leave.

I remember like it was yesterday when the truth finally came out! I had begun to receive messages from fake social media accounts telling me stuff that he was doing, which included pictures of a woman and inappropriate conversations. At that moment everything began to make sense and I had the proof I needed. Now I needed answers from him! This was the second time I was humiliated through social media and I was livid! My heart broke into a million pieces. When Tim called me on his lunch break, I told him everything I had found out and it left him no other choice but to come clean. Now everything made sense: Our limited conservations, him working so much and being glued to the phone. His first words were "I wanted to tell you so bad, but I knew when I did all of this would break your heart."

Yes, this heartbreak was caused by the man who vowed that he would NEVER hurt me! Who was this man? How could he be so stupid as to jeopardize everything we had worked for: our children, our happy home? That night sitting in the pitch dark on our living room couch with my crushed heart, I sat in disbelief as he talked on the phone. Never in a million years did I believe I'd have to deal with this! To make things even worse, I found out that my friends who were all around me, knew what was going on before I did.

I reminded him of the chances I had given him. How I had begged him time after time just to tell me rather than for me to hear it from somebody else. He had me walking around looking like a fool thinking my marriage was good while he was sleeping around and my so-called friends *knew*. I kept a lid on my embarrassment, anger and rage. Inside my emotions rattled and boiled. I thought I would explode. Oh he was surely going to pay for hurting me. One of the same church members who had smiled in my face was laying up with my husband! I was ready to storm that church and turn a few pews over!

Instead, I snapped as soon as he got home. I broke stuff and really tried to hurt him badly. I was mad at myself for ignoring all the early red flags. I was also angry about the foolishness that had been happening right under my nose that I also missed.

While Tim attempted to apologize, I heard nothing but my rage. I was so disgusted and hurt I couldn't stand the thought of looking at him or even being in the same room with him. To make matters worse we had just moved into a new home and we were in the middle of unpacking and trying to get settled. I was so ready to leave I began packing the kid's things preparing for my exit.

Tim broke down again trying to explain, pleading for me not to leave, just to hear him out. I listened to what he had to say but nothing mattered anymore. I was numb to everything. I didn't leave right then, but I stopped going to church and I isolated myself from everybody. I became robotic: I went to work and came home. As a result of being ashamed to go out in public, I became depressed and was really in a dark place. I tried to hang on for the sake of the kids but I knew they could tell something wasn't right with mommy and daddy.

Many days I didn't want to get out of bed, didn't want to eat and I just shut the whole world out. My babies saw Mommy many days just crying and they didn't know why. They would give me the biggest hugs providing a little push each day to keep me going. Eventually I called a good friend from Delaware and I cried and cried. I told her what was going on and she listened and not one time did she sugarcoat her words. She would say, "Don't focus on what you see, focus on the unseen because trouble is only temporary." Even though I didn't want to hear it, she told me to take my focus off him and the wrong he did and pray for my husband that God will deliver him and lead and guide us both through this all." At the end of our phone call she prayed for me. She sent me text messages to reflect on during this time.

God? Pray? What? I'm not praying! Why would I? God allowed this to happen to me. I was not trying to hear that! I was so angry because I thought I was doing all that a good wife was supposed to do and I still ended up heartbroken. I blamed myself. If I was skinny or perhaps if I had worn sexier clothes, maybe Tim wouldn't have cheated. Forget what my Delaware friend had said. I was leaving and I was taking the children with me. Had no clue where we would go, but I would figure it out.

That night I cried and hollered and cried some more. I asked God to let me die, the pain and humiliation was too much. Very clearly God said, "You can't leave, Tim needs you!" God showed me my broken husband and the issues he was dealing with. I cried even harder. How could I forgive and trust this man again? God said to me, "Just trust me."

Hurt and disgusted, I halfway trusted God to restore and heal my marriage. The days ahead were horrible. I flipped out every time I tried to talk to Tim, so I began avoiding any conversation with him at all. Every day he left for work I wondered if he was really there or just cheating again. I finally decided to search around for a counselor and in our very first counseling session I cried the entire time. I was a mess and I didn't think we would survive those sessions.

However we learned a lot about one another and ourselves and some toxic traits that we both had. Months passed and we continued with the counseling sessions as well as looking for a new church to attend. Things seemed to be looking good. Tim seemed to be putting forth every effort to regain my trust and I worked on myself and forgiveness.

Only I realized I didn't truly forgive him because I constantly reminded him every day of what he did. I verbally forgave him, but deep in my heart I had not really forgiven him. I would still cringe or get sick to my stomach if he even attempted to touch me. Tim would notice it but just brush it off. However I could see the hurt in his eyes because he was trying so hard on his end. As a result, my response toward him began to push him away and cause him to relive the feelings that had caused him to seek comfort outside of our marriage.

I didn't care! He was going to feel my pain. No I hadn't forgiven him. It was far easier to push all those thoughts and pain to the back of my head and not deal with it. Of course that wasn't possible. Once I saw his cheating partner and the thought of running her over with my car came to mind. It was at that moment I knew I needed help. Eventually I learned it wasn't right to continually bring his cheating up all the time and knowingly punish him over and over.

I had to forgive myself also and that was hard because I beat myself up every day. Bitter on the inside, pain began to impact my health and my children. Meanwhile, on the outside everything looked good and you would have had no idea the turmoil I was going through. I had to make a choice to wholeheartedly forgive my husband and mean it. This was by far the hardest thing that I ever had to go through, and I went through it alone because I had no one I could tell.

My family would have just made it worse and I didn't trust anyone because everyone had their own version of what was going on and the rumors were ridiculous. It was hard facing things alone, but I woke up every day determined to keep my sanity and take it day by day. At that point I had to forget what others were saying and focus on me and trust God to work out the rest. I had to heal and get help for myself.

The journey was difficult. I learned things about myself that I didn't necessarily like, but the lessons were needed. I'm thankful for my one good friend in Delaware that covered me in prayer and constantly checked on me. I always said something like this would never happen to me. I was that person who said, "If my spouse cheats on me, it's over." But when I was put in the situation, it was a different ballgame.

The process was long and difficult. Nothing happened overnight, but we managed to get through every day and become stronger. We both learned from our mistakes. Tim learned how to communicate with me when things were bothering him, and I learned that my family came first, everything else second. We learned to talk about everything and keep our communication open and honest.

Now we are approaching ten years of marriage. We will renew our vows later this year in front of family and friends with a strong foundation and God as our guide. We both had to put in work and set boundaries to make sure our marriage has a strong foundation. We are stronger and closer than ever. I never knew going through something like this and seeing each other at our weakest moments would bring us this close.

As a wife and mother, I regained my confidence and to this day I look in the mirror and speak over my life. My past doesn't define who I am now. I'm no longer ashamed of our story because we overcame. God restored our marriage and I'm forever grateful. God gave me a new love for my husband and the past three years have been the happiest I have ever been.

Perhaps we went through what we went through so we could help others. Together we birthed "Marriage Beyond Ministry" in October 2018. The business is a marriage group to promote balance, healthy and happy marriages, and to discuss real life issues. We plan date nights and other events to connect with other married couples. We're excited to present our very first marriage retreat this year! Without God none of this would have been possible. As part of the business, I was led to obtain certification as a life coach. We opened "Becoming a Better You, LLC" in February 2020 which offers life and marriage coaching. Tim and I are living witnesses that God can bring restoration to a marriage after infidelity. The road to forgiveness takes hard work, but is possible after betrayal.

DISCOVERING THE GIFTS OF ME

By: Janet L. Jacobs

You are so dumb. Can't you do anything right? You are good for nothing. No one has ever wanted you. Look at you! You're fat, you're too skinny, you talk funny, you are single with four kids, you're ugly, you're clumsy. You can't make it without me. You need me. You better be thankful you got that man, don't mess this one up.

Listen to that, do you hear it; the words keep reverberating in my head. Those words creep in several times a day in the back of my mind waiting their turn to speak, even when I'm sleeping. Although different people have said these things to me over the span of my lifetime, I keep hearing the words replayed over and over. Somehow this has become my new normal. How did I get here?

The best thing to ever happen to me besides my children was my paternal Grandmother. She raised me as her own and I called her Mommy. She stepped in with her daughter and other relatives to raise me. It was mostly unheard of for the paternal side to raise a child but I am forever grateful. It was she and I, and she did the best for me that she could.

We did everything together. I went to church, shopped, watched television and cooked with her. There were also chores, schoolwork, fun times and sad times, typical family stuff. However, there was always something missing. I often felt out of place, left out and thrown away because my mother wasn't in my life. I saw cousins and friends being raised with at least one parent if not two in the same house. The feeling wasn't jealousy, but a feeling of wanting someone to love me. Did I do something wrong?

I thought maybe if I just kept quiet and out of the way, if I became invisible, maybe someone would come for me. It is crazy that up until a little while ago as this was being written, I was still waiting. The feelings of being inadequate and never being good enough seems to never go away.

The feeling of being abandoned by my biological mother is one of the reasons I have always felt different. I was dumped and forgotten while others were kept. There is so much depth and many layers to my hurt. There were other factors as well that stripped me. On several occasions, I was inappropriately touched and kissed as a child by someone deemed trustworthy. I felt that it was not right but as a child, you really don't know what to do. The touches and kisses did not feel right. I finally shared what was happening with a friend; incidentally, her mother was dating my abuser, my uncle. I heard a bunch of yelling, crying and arguing and I was so scared. My friend's mother was screaming at my uncle from their apartment next door and then she came to see my Grandmother. My Grandmother asked me and I told her. I thought I was going to be sent away but nothing else was said. To my knowledge, the authorities were not called and soon after, we moved to another state. Even after the abuse came to light, I now know it was swept under the rug. My guess is my complaints weren't taken as seriously because he "only touched" me.

In another incident, as a budding teenager, another distant relative touched my breast in plain view of others at a family gathering and it drew laughter and a playful, "leave her alone!" The horror, embarrassment, and utter humiliation that I felt then, still brings tears to my eyes. This incident along with previous abuse is one of the reasons why I am not big on hugging or random physical affection.

Church was a big part of my life; just about, all of my immediate family went to the same church. We did the usual Sunday School, Bible Study, Choir Practice twice a week, Usher Board Practice, and other church events, it was a real community sadly missed in this day and time. Junior high school was great! I had a "boyfriend" I was really fond of. We were young and limited, so our dates consisted of missing the bus on purpose, going to Friendly's for ice cream and walking home, talking and laughing all the way. Holding hands in the hallways, walking me to class and meeting after school were a few things we enjoyed. We were allowed to go to church and have supervised visits.

Everything was very innocent. The school year went by quickly and the first year of high school began. I was active in school clubs, activities and sports. Even with all of my activities, it was still awkward to fit in because of my trust issues but also of what people thought of me. On the home front as a teenager, life became uneasy as my abuser uncle moved into our house. I could not understand why and how that happened. It was clear that he abused me as a child but now here he was in my home, where was supposed to feel safe. As a defense mechanism, I started dating an older boyfriend with a car. I stayed out late and remained away from home as often as I could.

More labels and taunts came after that, "She's fast, she's loose, look at the church girl doing those things." It was t hen that survival mode took over. If I was going to have sex, I would have rather it be with my boyfriend instead of my uncle, who had sworn we could run away, get married and have babies. My uncle insinuating such things made my skin crawl and made me feel like trash.

On the one hand, somebody other than my Grandmother finally wanted me – but in an unnatural way. What should have been a joyful, memorable senior year rite of passage ended up being clouded in shame, insecurity, hurt and anger. My uncle attacked me the night before my prom. I called the authorities and alerted family members but once again, nothing was done. "I told you she's lying, she's making it up, she's 'fast." My uncle ended up marrying a friend of mine with a similar name to cover up his devious acts. Again, he got away with it.

About a year later when I was almost nineteen, my Grandmother moved out into her own apartment and my cousins and I rented the house. I graduated high school, was an adult, working and taking care of myself. We had great times navigating life. One was older and the other was younger and I was in the middle. It was not perfect but it was the beginning of being responsible. We worked but had room for fun. We hosted card parties, fight parties (Mike Tyson was the rage), and holiday get-togethers with our friends.

I felt some type of freedom from my church girl status because I started experimenting with alcohol and had already started smoking a few years ahead. I had sneaked cigarettes at 14 so I knew how. I made some mistakes, one in particular I regret to this day, but I thought I was grown and it was the right thing to do.

During this time, I became engaged to a guy I met and had been dating for a while. Someone wanted me permanently! I totally ignored what I now know were red flags, because I was so happy that someone wanted me. I found myself grasping to belong to something or someone. It turned out to be a different experience than I thought it would be. After the engagement, I decided to move to Brooklyn to live with my fiancé. Such a big step but I was just running away towards something new. Brooklyn was a different world compared to Long Island. I felt like an alien trying to adjust. I just couldn't believe that people lived that close together on purpose with no yards. However, subways and corner stores were in abundance and nobody ever went to bed.

We settled into life as young people in our twenties. Things were not perfect but we both worked. We went out to eat, attended movies and concerts, shopped and just lived life with no one telling us what to do. He gave wonderful gifts – Belgium roses, Godiva chocolates, limo rides, singing telegrams and we attended block parties and other events. It was awesome. I was introduced to things I had never experienced before.

Before long, something changed. He became controlling and before I knew it, I was in a situation less than stellar. Something inside me knew it was wrong but being young, I believed the man should control the household. I quickly fell into the routine of accepting whatever happened to me. I tiptoed through the days/nights trying not to make any waves and stayed quiet. The abusive words and slaps became volatile.

"Don't leave this house, don't answer the phone, just lay here and be in the same spot when I get back. "I can tell if you move and if you do, I'll bust you upside your head."

"You leaving me, huh? Where are you going, nobody wants you."

"What took you so long to get home, where have you been?"

Those hurtful words began to pepper my thoughts again. I wasn't good enough, I should be grateful to have someone. The physical abuse continued along with emotional. Each incident would come out of nowhere at times. I felt that this was how it was supposed to be. This went on for years and he had no control over himself, even hitting me in front of his parents. I became pregnant and everything went back to like when we were dating and first married. Suddenly he was so nice to me and caring. It was a beautiful experience. He began attending medical appointments, Lamaze classes and he made plans with me for our baby.

EVOLVE

Our beautiful and perfect daughter was born. Although parenthood and working were stressful, I truly enjoyed it. It was short-lived though, as the abuse picked back up and after a sudden death in the family, it got even worse. Even walking in the neighborhood became a problem. I was told to keep my eyes down and if I made eye contact with a man, he would say I had to know him and it was a problem once we got home and I knew what would follow… more berating and beatings. I thought this was going to be my life from now on.

Then I became pregnant a second time and another beautiful and perfect daughter arrived. One day, I summed up enough strength to talk back and defend myself because the control and threats was directed towards the two things I loved more than anything - my babies. I decided that day to leave. I left my Park Avenue job, packed two suitcases and walked away. Shout out to my day-care provider, I will never forget her. When I quietly paid her double, she knew what to do. She put aside the other half in an envelope for me. When it was time to go, she gave me back my envelope and the money helped a lot towards a new start.

Safely back around family, we lived with their help and I managed to get back on my feet. It was hard with a

9-month old and a 21-month old. It was stressful and as a result I picked up drinking, smoking and excessive eating. I was able to find work and navigate childcare while using public transportation. During this time, my Grandmother's twenty-plus-year prayer was answered. She had prayed for this just about every night since I was a little girl. I was finally able to meet my biological mother. She came because I, along with the help of my father, purchased her ticket.

Earlier plans at 14-years-old did not happen as I felt the terms of meeting did not feel comfortable. I did not want to go without my Grandmother. So now, at twenty-seven years old, I didn't quite know how to act. Physically laying eyes on her, hearing her, being in the same room with her was surreal. When we met it was around the holidays and I finally had both parents in the same room as my father came by. I felt five-years-old again. Scared relief is what I felt. Nervousness took over to the point where I was almost numb. I had always searched for answers but still do not have them. My mother's response to any question was that she did what she thought was best. Those words always stung because she did not call or ask for me. I am thankful and grateful to have had my Grandmother and my father's family.

The somewhat good feeling was short-lived for my beloved Grandmother passed away four months later. The devastation and brokenness resides with me today. I feel that if I had not arranged to meet my mother, I would have had more time with my Grandmother...she prayed the prayer to live long enough for me to meet her.

After attempting to reconcile with my husband on my terms (staying in Long Island), I soon discovered that this was the wrong thing to do. The abuse started back up and the trust and feelings of self-worth went to the toilet. The marriage ended. I was alone with the girls for a while and was introduced to someone I briefly knew as a teenager. We talked and began dating and this new relationship resulted in me having a handsome son and a tiny, but strong little girl.

There was never physical abuse, but the relationship was emotionally and mentally challenging. Our son had physical delays and our daughter was premature. It was a struggle but God and others saw us through. It was so tiring being a mother of four young children. What kept me going was the fact that I knew what it felt like not to have my mother there for me and I could not give up. I often thought suicide was the answer, but could not think of what would become of the children.

My Grandmother and Aunt were everything to me, but I had to make it for these children. I strived to give them me; it may not have been ideal for most, but we had what we had. I was determined to raise them and not leave them. I knew what it was like to be left and did not wish that for them. Over the years, we experienced having to move often, not living in the most ideal places but I strived to keep them in an ideal school district.

I experienced extreme depression and wanted to hurt myself. I often dreamed about what would happen to my children if they didn't have me around. I went through a hospitalization for a nervous breakdown and ended up separated from my children. I didn't know what to feel and could not imagine what they must have felt during my hospital stay. With the help of prayer from the senior mentors of my church, and upon hearing the stress in my children's voices when I called them on a payphone, I was able to convince the hospital to let me go with the promise of attending an out-patient program to be able to keep the children together and for the State not to split them up. The letters they wrote were profound and they sounded mature above their years; I have those letters today and often read them. They prayed for me to get better and promised to give everyone my best – they were showing the strength I did not have at that moment. I knew I had to do better.

I went home and the children joined me. It wasn't easy but I will say the children are what pulled me through. I regret putting them in a grown-up situation and having them feel responsible for the household. Honestly, the four of them were my reason for staying alive. They were my hope. They gave me what no one else could give me: a reason to live.

Once back home, the gossip started again, "Gosh, look at her! She makes it seem easy. Don't talk to her! She's crazy! She thinks she is better than everyone! Do you know what she said? I can't stand her! She makes me sick. Why does he like her?"

Again, the voices reverberated, recorded for perpetual playback in my mind. Life had its highs and lows. Car, no car, cabs everywhere, limited activities, some days eating less but eating none-the-less. Having to ask for help and being looked down upon. I did not qualify for public assistance because I worked; it felt like I was being penalized because I wanted to work.

I can't stress the positive impact that my daycare providers had on us. My last one practically raised the kids and, in a sense, me as well. They always looked out for us and are still in touch with us today. The two fathers were in and out but mostly out of the children's lives. Due to their instability, we made do with what we had. I tried to work a second job but it took too much time away and it put a lot of pressure on the oldest to help. I resigned to make it work on one salary and it was not always enough but God sent Angels that were always on time.

After another long-term relationship ended in abuse, I ended up in therapy because I chose me. I kept my family back together and was piecing out some happiness and stability. But once again, I was so closed in and practically a recluse because of the brokenness and trust issues I experienced. I would not attend family functions and barely left the house. Unannounced visitors were an absolute no-no. Many times, the door or telephone remained unanswered.

With regained confidence and through the urging of a cousin, I struck up a virtual friendship with someone from my early adult years and we became friends and confidants. He, too, had struggles and hard times. We talked on the phone for several months but not one romantic thing was said. I continued in therapy and we continued to be friends. I talked so negatively about men in general, almost forgetting he was a man himself.

He begged me not to give up on men. I stated I had no interest in women but resigned to be alone for the rest of my life due to trust issues, hurt from abuse, rejection and just plain old disappointment. Again, he asked me not to give up on men. Incredulously I asked, "Who, you?" It never crossed my mind that I would want to try again. For some reason, my heart gave in to love again and we started a relationship.

With all that I've experienced in my life, the thought of being in a relationship let alone marrying again was definitely scary. I was okay with being companions, living out the rest of our lives together, until he proposed! I was surprised, happy and in utter shock at the same time. Those thoughts again, swirling in the back of my mind put a block on my willingness to go forward with marriage. First of all, did I even deserve this? Is this the right time? What if he's like the rest? I thought I was 100% healed and ready to move forward.

Relationships are hard when you both still carry unhealed issues. My past taught me what I did not want in a relationship. We moved forward and married. Life is good and it has highs and lows, ups and downs, good and bad situations. I can be funny but still reserved, closed in at times and in a rare moment, feel free enough to embrace it all.

My unresolved traumas from abandonment, abuse and trust gives me more labels - standoffish, distrusting, angry, stubborn, staying quiet to keep the peace and avoid dealing with an issue, nervous, sad, scared and at times, alone. It causes issues in my marriage and it takes time and a lot of communication to get through the struggles. I feel my current marriage is good because we were friends first.

What I feel is not so good is my tug of war with feelings and how to express them. Some feelings and situations will cause me to completely shut down because I don't want to deal with them. I do not have a problem talking, but at times the way I want to express myself and how I actually do it are totally different. That scared little girl steps forward, and I am instantly quiet; or the rebellious "fast" teen comes out. Sometimes the young single mother stuck in survival mode comes out; and lastly, the "can't nobody get over on me, I don't need you," woman comes out. At times, it is a combination of them all, but my husband and I are in this together. His struggles are mine and vice versa. Some will understand and some won't, hell, sometimes I don't understand.

I am still a work in progress; but I'll end with this - a love letter to myself. I've never written a love letter to myself before because it's never been about me. But I'm about to change that.

Dear Janet: What I want to say to you is that you've always felt like you were encased in a bubble with life going on around you in a haze, navigating life, raising kids, working a job and taking care of others. It's what you do and have always done to feel like you belong. When will you know that you are good enough for you? That you are talented and deserve everything that life has to offer.

Janet, it is not your fault you were abandoned, felt awkward and alone, teased about being skinny, fat, that you were assaulted, and you were promiscuous. It was not your fault you were beaten, abused, lied to and forced into survival mode. You did the right thing by keeping the children together which is more than your birth mother did. You are a wonderful strong woman, you are talented. You can and will succeed. You will no longer allow negative thoughts in your mind to keep you stagnant. See, know and believe what others already know about you. Trust what God has put inside of you and more importantly, trust yourself. You are no longer the little girl, waiting. Release the hurt and put that energy elsewhere, no longer allowing isolation to hinder you, your growth, your potential, your attitude and who YOU are. The hardships of resentment, abandonment and forgiveness are in the past. Step forward, and no longer listen to the voices in the back of your head, for the final voice is YOURs. For the love YOU seek is already in you. Allow YOU to come to the front. The approval YOU seek is inside YOU and lastly, the gifts are there for you to discover; it is your choice.

Love Always,

The Ever - Evolving Woman

Matthew 6:34 - Therefore, do not worry about tomorrow, for tomorrow will worry about itself. Each day has enough trouble of its own.

NOTHING BUT A MIRACLE

By: Shania Elliott-McDowell

Hearing the words, "You can't have any more children," my heart dropped to the floor. All sorts of thoughts ran through my mind, "Is he going to leave me now? How is he going to feel? Would he want to marry me knowing that I can't give him what he always wanted?"

What was I to do? How was I going tell him? Was this going to crush his whole world? I remember going home and sitting in the room by myself, grappling with the idea of not being able to have any more children. I didn't feel like a woman, I felt empty inside. I think I remained in the room alone in the dark just staring into space asking God for an explanation. I cried until I couldn't cry anymore. He would ask me what was wrong and why. It took me almost two weeks to tell him exactly what the Doctor told me.

My children and I moved to Charlotte, NC from New York in the summer of 2007. My friend Tamika decided to put up an online dating profile of me. I remember her saying I needed to "get out there." I wasn't interested in dating or getting to know anyone. I was recently divorced from my first husband, but she kept bugging me, so I let her go ahead and do it.

I remember receiving my first couple of replies. Steve was one of them. He was good looking and single, so I decided to send a reply back. He responded and we chatted for about as long as the day permitted us to talk via yahoo messenger. I intended to give him my number so I could hear how he sounded on the phone because you can tell a lot about a person by their voice. We talked on the phone every day after that until he suggested we meet in person.

I will never forget the day we met. He came to my house after I got out of class. There he stood with a look I never seen before, like, *she was going to be my wife.* We talked outside as if we had known one another forever. He asked me on a date, and I said yes. We went on a couple of dates afterward and we enjoyed spending time together. Time flew by so fast as we dated. The next thing I wanted him to do was to meet my children. He met them, and my children liked him from the start. I guess they saw that I was happy. I remember when we initially discussed having children. I was so adamant about not having any more children because my daughter was born with medical issues. Steve didn't have any children and I knew he wanted at least one. So, I was afraid my unwillingness to have more was going to be a problem.

In my mind, we were still dating. I wasn't that serious with him yet. We hadn't said anything about being in a committed relationship and he was ready to discuss kids. So, you know what I did? I left him alone for a while. I ignored his calls and didn't respond to his texts. I was scared. This was moving way too fast. We continued to talk and take things slow for the next year or so and by 2009, we became more serious and we met each other's families.

Around this time, we both knew what we wanted and we were committed to making our relationship work. On this one particular weekend, we made plans to visit his father and stepmom. I had everything set up. I was about to make a great thing happen or make the biggest mistake of my life. I was going to ask Steve to be my husband. Before I did it, I went into the bathroom and gave myself a pep talk. Then it was time. Yes, I know it was unorthodox for the woman to ask the man. However, I knew we both wanted to propose, I just moved a little faster. We were supposed to be together. He said yes. All the way home he stared at that ring and just smiled. When we got home, he was still shocked. "OH MY GOD!!! This woman actually proposed and waited. I said YES!!!"

I knew at some point the question was going to come up again and it did by the end of the week. I didn't care if we were lying in the bed or walking to the store. All I kept hearing was, "When are you going to be ready to give me a baby?" "SHANIA, I think it's time for us to talk about another baby." In my mind I said okay let's try, but my heart was saying no we are not ready. Let's enjoy ourselves first. The kids were almost out of the house and we will be alone. I said him, "Let's just enjoy this engagement and see what the future holds."

Everything was going great until the end of that year when my father's health started going downhill. In

EVOLVE

February, 2010, my dad passed away. His passing was the hardest times of my entire life. I lost my dad, and the man I wanted to marry wasn't there for me. Have you ever had to go through something so terrifying alone? Well, I did. I had to go through my dad's wake and a funeral without his physical presence. The only support I received was a verbally expressed, "It will be okay."

Later that year my mother broke both her legs and my struggle continued. Happy New Year! It's 2011. We drove my mom back to New York after the Christmas Holidays. It was early that morning when we got to my mom's house. Steve, my mom, and my children planned for him to propose to me with my kids standing in for my dad. It was so romantic him down on one knee and my children standing behind him.

A couple of months later, the first pregnancy happened, or so I thought. I went two months with no cycle and the Doctor kept telling me I wasn't pregnant. I went to my GYN and she did an ultrasound, telling me I was carrying a fetus in my fallopian tube. She was surprised that it hadn't ruptured my tube. She gave me medicine to have the fetus pass. That was the most horrifying ordeal outside of giving birth, and it wouldn't be the last.

In March 2012 we got married, one of the happiest days of my life. Two months after sharing a happy time, we lost my father-in-law. We also had another pregnancy scare. I didn't even realize I was suffering a miscarriage because so much was going on. My husband started closing us out due to his father passing and being newly married. I was becoming mentally and physically drained from trying to be his support and support for my children.

I fell into a depression I couldn't give this man, my new husband, what he always wanted. He would say it was okay, but I knew it bothered him. All of his friends had children of their own, and while he had mine, it just wasn't the same. We both decided that we would stop trying and if it was God's will for us to have a child, then we would. I took this time to concentrate on my school work, my children, and my job. He took this time to work through his own depression. He went back to school. Everyone was busy doing something and things were getting back to what I would consider normal.

Two years had passed. I said to myself that I am getting up there in age so if I wanted to have a child, I needed to start trying again now. I worked at a gynecologist's office so I asked my doctors what were good strategies for getting pregnant. They told me many different ways to try and conceive. Being that my cycle was completely out of whack and I suffered from endometriosis, it would be difficult. We tried everything from me in a handstand to lying propped up on pillows, nothing worked. Frustration set in so I said, let's go to the doctor. The day we decided to go is when my world went from happy to devastating. First was my husband's appointment. They told him everything was okay with him so it was my turn to see the doctor. When the Doctor came into the room, for some reason it felt like the room suddenly got dark and grew cold.

"Shania, do you remember when you had that ectopic pregnancy," the doctor asked?
I nodded. The doctor continued, "Well one of your Fallopian tubes is completely torn, and the other has scar tissue."

All I heard was the air hitting the window and all I saw was his mouth moving as my world-shattered. He also said there was no way that I would be able to have any more children.

"Shania, Shania," was all I recall him repeating, "You okay?" I said, "Yes Doc I guess I'm as okay as I am going to be."

He handed me a variety of different pamphlets on infertility with other options to have children. In my mind, I was saying who wants this shit? But somehow, I managed to mouth the words, "Thank you." When you are expecting a positive outcome and you get a whole different answer, what are you supposed to say? How do you come back from this? I got in my car and went home and continued with my day like I hadn't just received the worst news ever.

My day moved so slowly, all I wanted to do was cry and cry some more. I went home and avoided everyone. After those two weeks had passed, I finally told my husband what the doctor had told me. I saw the tears well up in his eyes and the hurt creep upon his face as he tried to hold it all together for me. I showed him the pamphlets, and he looked at me the same way I felt about the pamphlets when I received them.

The next day I got up and went to work. The Doctor I worked with came to me and said, "I have some hope for you. He said there is a place I think can help you. They offer different types of treatment for what you are going through." That afternoon, I told my husband about the infertility clinic the doctor mentioned. They were having a meet and greet and we should go.

There we met all of the doctors. There was one in particular that stood out from the rest. He came over to us and introduced himself personally. He said he'd been with the clinic for a couple of years and asked if we had any questions. We went over everything this clinic had to offer and how the process worked for each treatment offered. Then he gave us another pamphlet with the price for each treatment. I wanted to break down and cry because the prices were so outrageous for our budget. But my husband seemed optimistic and said if this is what we want, we will make a way for it.

We made an appointment to begin the invitro-fertilization. On paper it looked like a quick and easy process. On our first couple of appointments we had to give blood and take urine samples. I didn't mind even though I am deathly afraid of needles. The next step involved taking the birth control pill for a month or two to regulate my cycle. Have you ever been on a high dose of the birth control pill? What an emotional rollercoaster! I would cry, be happy and angry all at the same time! After that month, I had to start giving myself hormones through needles to enlarge my eggs. Once they were at the correct size, my Doctor extracted the eggs by ultrasound. That process was a little easier than I initially thought.

The next step was the fertilization process that took a week. As I waited, I gave myself more hormones to prep my body for when the embryos would be ready to be placed. That week felt like a whole eternity. They called to let you know how many viable embryos were created. That week I waited for the office to call. I went back to work because staying home was driving me crazy. Upon my arrival, I found an envelope on my desk. I opened it and there was a check to pay for the rest of my procedure and a gift card.

I had a moment and I wanted to hug my doctors. I was ecstatic because they didn't have to do this for me, but they did. They had already started praying for me as well. The tears rolled down my face. I would be forever thankful to them for their generosity and thoughtfulness.

The big day arrived: embryo placement. I was so nervous. Our doctor assured me that everything was going to be okay. We watched him place three of my embryos back into my uterus and the waiting game began.

EVOLVE

As we prayed for at least one of the embryos to take root in my womb, I continued giving myself the shots. I was told to wait a week before testing by the third day in that week I was becoming anxious, I went and purchased all the pregnancy test I could think of. I took the first one and three minutes felt like an ETERNITY, but it was time and so went to look. POSITIVE, my pregnancy test came back positive! I called my husband and told him I had something to say to him. He said, "What is it?" I said, "We're pregnant." I think he started crying. I know I did. When we went to the doctor, we had to do an ultrasound, and there it was! The little heartbeat we had been waiting for!

This pregnancy was the hardest pregnancy that I had to endure. At first, it was the shots through large needles that I had to administer throughout the pregnancy. Then there was bleeding during my first trimester which caused me to be on bed rest. Then I almost delivered the baby too early and had to get a cerclage, or barrier, placed against my uterus for me to make it to my ninth month. Finally, the last month of my trimester was here, I thanked God almost every day because I was so ready to give birth. I was almost ready to deliver the baby myself.

Then just as we were preparing for my first baby shower and getting everything together, my husband's mother passed away. That was the hardest thing he had to deal with in life. Everything stopped for a couple of weeks because Steve went into a deep depression, withdrawing from me and the pregnancy for a while.

On May 29, 2015 at 2:11p.m., our baby boy arrived. At 7lbs and 11ozs, he was so perfect with ten toes, ten fingers, four limbs and screaming as loudly as possible. I never thought I'd be a mother again yet here I am starting all over again with this little person. Would I do everything I endured in order to have that precious bundle in my life? YES!

I love watching him grow and discovering new things through his eyes! He is so wonderful and is nothing but a miracle. Throughout this experience, I found myself evolving from the heartbreak of thinking I would never be able to give my wonderful husband the child he'd always dreamed of, to the joy of being able to bestow biological fatherhood to my husband through our marriage bond, making our little family complete.

MY 9-1-1 MOMENT

By: Michelle W. Pennington

Where to begin? I can't even tell you how humbled and excited I am at the same time, to both share my story and - let's face it - get some things off my chest. My name is Michelle Pennington. I've been married to my husband for six years and we've been together for twelve. We jokingly say we've been married since the day we met so let's go with twelve years for the purpose of this story.

When my now husband and I met, I was still married to my first husband. I know what you're thinking. I would have given myself the side-eye as well. Truth be told, my marriage had been flatlining for quite some time and was one nail in the coffin from being declared dead.

Did I make mistakes? Sure, I did. Did I contribute to the overall downfall of the marriage? Absolutely. I'm not blaming my first husband for anything or any more than I blame myself for. I was in control of my actions, I was an adult and I'll be honest, I was a bit reckless. That saying 'young, dumb, and full of cum' described me to a T. I felt life had 'shorted' me of what I really wanted, so I set out to get what I felt I deserved.

My first husband and I were college sweethearts. We met on campus via mutual friends at the tender ages of nineteen and twenty-one. There weren't sparks immediately as we both were dating other people. However, we did recognize the other as attractive and worthy of getting to know better. As time passed our relationship grew from strictly friendly to romantic.

We spent quite a lot of time together and realized we had several common denominators: mutual family structure, career goals, aspirations for our future, and most importantly we enjoyed each other's company. What I was too blind to see were some red flags, nothing major in the beginning. I assumed what I didn't like would change. In reality that rarely ever happens and it didn't happen for me either. I was having fun, despite the red flags and wanted to continue to ride my high.

EVOLVE

I don't remember there being any fancy pomp and circumstance but one day it just seemed we had fallen into a relationship and were happily dating. We completed school together, each of us graduating with our undergraduate degrees in Communications. In love and recently finished with school, we felt like we could conquer the world. It was only a few months after graduating that we got married and proceeded down the yellow brick road to what we thought would be our happy ending.

The first few years were as normal as apple pie. We did all the traditional things a newly married couple would do. We bought a house, had a baby, got a dog and a white picket fence for the dog. Our careers were taking off and we were gaining ground in our industries. We had lots of friends, our families loved us, and all was well…on the outside.

There were a few aspects of our lives that were private. The first being that I noticed my husband began struggling to walk and keep his balance. There was nothing glaring at first, a trip here, or a subtle stumble there. I just assumed he was getting a little clumsy or needed an adjustment to his eyeglass prescription. I wrote it off as something correctible. However, after a few years, the condition didn't go away or even get better, it actually got worse, much worse.

The second issue in our marriage was our spiritual relationship. When confronted with his medical crisis it was natural for me to turn to God, the church, and its leaders for help and guidance. However, this created a divide in our home as my husband adamantly disagreed with this approach. We had been raised on opposite ends of the religion spectrum and it was obvious this would be a perpetual point of contention.

Lastly, there was my desire to have more children. I didn't want my baby to be an only child like I was growing up. I wanted more than anything for her to have siblings, people close to her own age who could be supportive. In a nutshell, we had some issues.

As years passed, my husbands' physical condition worsened. He was in denial that anything was wrong so taking suggestions from me as to how to handle it was met with disdain. Meanwhile, it was difficult for him to work which made our financial life unstable. That led to him being angry most of time which was the catalyst for some pretty heated and frequent debates. To add, we had no spiritual connection to each other or any house of worship. As a unit, "we" were spiraling out of control.

While my husband was deteriorating in front of me and not taking his condition seriously, I pushed on. I carried the responsibilities: the house, the baby, the finances, you name it - I took care of it, and my bitterness grew. After all, I was a twenty-something professional with serious ambition and my husband was continuously out of work and increasingly 'ok' with it. My resentment turned to anger. How dare he put all of the responsibility on me? I felt like I had two children: him and our baby, and no husband. The life I had imagined for myself was rapidly disappearing. This sucked, and I was raging mad!

After years of anguish, my selfish nature rose to the surface. I was young, attractive, and by now my career was on a steady incline. I was taking care of everything at home and I didn't feel the need to abide by traditional marital rules. I worked all the time, came home late, traveled often (alone) and as my friends called it, 'I was behaving single.' They were right.

I didn't want to be married anymore. I communicated my feelings to my husband. He was displeased and combative and thought I was seriously over-reacting. He did not share my viewpoint, nor did he see our marriage as problematic. He felt as though we had some issues but nothing that couldn't be resolved. I, on the other hand, was well past wanting to reconcile. I was sick and tired of being sick and tired. Seeing my overall frustration, he conceded the fight and we separated. However, he clearly let it be known to me and everyone we knew that he disapproved and that this was my decision. I was destroying our family and he was simply 'going along with it.'

Upon his departure I felt like a new person, lighter. I didn't have this gloomy cloud hanging over my head. An inner peace found me that I hadn't experienced in a long time. The need to create circumstances to keep me out of the house were now gone. I could move freely, without answering to anyone. I had my life back. But my husband hadn't given up. He was adamantly opposed to divorce and assumed I would eventually 'come to my senses' and everything could go back to the way it was. I on the other hand, assumed my wishes were clear and although not well received, were understood. I was wrong. I was hoping for an amicable divorce between two consenting adults, but I didn't get anything close to that. Little did I know I would be in for years of back-and-forth. Separated, then not, then separated again. It was a roller coaster ride and not a fun one.

Then, during one of our many on-again-off-again periods, I met my current husband in what some would call, and 'unconventional manner.' He was a professional singer on tour and I worked as a sales manager at a radio station. One night a well-known artist came to town to perform and my radio station hosted the after-party. A sea of celebrities and music industry executives milled about the room. This was nothing new for me. Having worked at a radio station, and previously in TV, rubbing elbows with famous people was a common occurrence.

As I was leaving the bar and returning to my group with what was likely our third round of drinks, I ran right into my husband, literally. I spilled the drinks on him, the bar, and the floor. Embarrassed, I immediately apologized, but the damage was done. I had ruined his jacket. He was an incredibly good sport about it and laughed it off.

In an attempt to make amends, I offered to dry clean the jacket and I gave him my business card so he could contact me on Monday. He didn't contact me Monday, Tuesday, Wednesday, or anytime that week, so I assumed it wasn't a big deal to him and I wouldn't hear from him. Instead, he called me two weeks later, no mention of the jacket. We talked for hours and that's when I knew he was special. We continued the conversation for weeks which lead to months. Each conversation grew in intensity and after four months of phone calls, texts, and emails, we finally met in person for just the second time.

It was soon after that second encounter that I realized I was falling in love with this man and that was terrifying because I was still legally married to my husband. Out of all of the big events in my life up to this point, nothing compared to the anxiety I felt about telling my family about my precarious situation. I had married, had a baby, suffered a couple miscarriages, graduated from college, bought several houses, started new jobs and earned promotions, experienced close family deaths, but THIS was different. This was not only going to be extremely tough it was also going to be controversial. I knew the judgement my conservative family would heap on me. They would consider me an adulterer, a cheater or worse and I didn't want to be labeled. But I couldn't turn my heart off and I didn't want to.

The months following were simultaneously some of the happiest and saddest times in my life. I was juggling too many emotions. I was ecstatic to have found companionship but the timing was less than ideal.

Trying to keep everything balanced weighed heavily on me. I cried often, bursting into tears at the most inappropriate times. Before walking into a meeting the tears would hit and I'd have to instantly get myself together. Keeping busy helped my mind from going to dark places, so I intentionally kept my calendar 'dance mom full.' So full in fact that I was only home to sleep, shower, and shit.

Anything and everything I could do to keep my mind off of the inevitable, I did. The uncomfortable conversation I had been avoiding was telling my husband that I definitely wanted a divorce. Avoidance was working, but the results wreaked havoc on my life. Maybe if I didn't see him or talk to him much, he would just 'go away.' He never disappeared and it had come time to let him know our marriage had to end.

Then there was my family. I knew they would disapprove of how I had met my boyfriend and that we continued to interact while I was still married. They were, and still are, an extremely conservative group of people. I longed to have a sibling or cousins close to my age who I could confide in and maybe gain another perspective. I wanted to be able to tell someone in my family what I was going through and selfishly solicit confirmation for my actions.

Thankfully, I had great friends and they were my strength, my voice of reason and they added calm to my chaos. They were supportive and direct, calling me out on my shenanigans and giving me a hug when I needed it. I wasn't naïve to what I was doing. Let's call it what it was, I was having an affair. I internally rationalized and justified my feelings and wrestled with how to communicate my state of mind to my family and my first husband. It was something that kept me up at night, tossing and turning, and giving me nightmares on a regular basis. I was conflicted to my core. How on earth would I tell them what I had done without losing all of their respect and facing a tsunami of judgement?

After nearly a year of procrastinating, I reached my breaking point and it was time to confess my position to my family. I knew that me cheating on and divorcing my husband would be looked upon as a 'black eye' on the family and would be met with shame and disgust, but it had to be done. I was now out of time. My actions had caught up to me. I was pregnant by a man who was not my husband. Given the timing I was confident who the father was. While I was looking forward to having this little baby, telling my then- husband about it would be awkward, but telling my family would be mortifying. I had to deliver the unbelievable news that not only had I been in a relationship with a man who was not my husband for months, but I was expecting his "love child."

Some images and experiences you never forget. I remember exactly where I was and what I was doing the moment the first plane struck New York City on September 11, 2001. That was a defining moment in my life. On the one hand there was my pre-9/11 life and on the other there was my post-9/11 life. The World Trade Center tragedy was an event so inconceivable that it changed the world.

Telling my family about my situation was like my personal 9/11 moment. Speaking with them and 'coming clean' about what was happening in my life meant things could never go back the way they were before the impending conversation. Their opinion of me would change. I would be viewed differently. The sky would fall, so I braced for impact. I asked everyone over for dinner, hoping the food would help pacify the response. My intent was to get it out before the meal was over but to no avail. After dinner we gathered in the living room. I told myself this has to be it, this has to be the moment you stand up and let them know the truth.

I spoke my piece, hoping to lead to my peace. My words broke with tears. I experienced every named emotion. Then finally, it was over. I had said what I needed to say. Everyone knew. The weight lifted, I awaited a response. The obstinate moment of silence following my total and complete confession felt eternal. I felt like I was in The Matrix and, preparing to dodge all the bullets soon coming my way. All eyes on me, I stood there trying to reconcile within myself what just happened. I'm sure my family suffered from information overload. In actuality there was probably only a few seconds between me finishing my last statement and someone breaking the silence.

Shock and awe is the only way I can properly describe their reaction. It was a lot to take in. Again, my family was and still is mostly conservative, so my behavior went well beyond anything they could've imagined. For most of my life I knew I was different from them. I was the youngest, I was more of a rebel, I was more dangerous, more willing to take risks, the most likely to leave home and never return. They knew I was spontaneous because I always had been. In lay terms, I was messy. And I feared what I just revealed to them played into that perception and I was probably right. My family didn't react with hugs, kisses, and well wishes, they reacted with scrutiny and a barrage of questions. The gravity of the situation, immediately evident. My hope of things 'going well' extinguished, and they successfully reminded me of the horror of my new reality. I was the official black sheep and I knew it.

That was a long night and one I wouldn't wish on anyone. Emotionally painful, mentally exhausting and physically debilitating, I could feel my body breaking down from the stress of the verbal exchanges. After I-don't-know-how-many hours my family left and I was alone. My 9/11 moment just happened and I had several questions looming in my head, the most poignant being "what do I do now?" Then I remembered a friend's supporting words, 'this too shall pass.' I clung to the notion that somehow "this" would pass, too and my life could reconvene as usual.

That night left me raw, vulnerable, and exposed. It was a defining moment for me. I had to 'put my big girl panties on' because I was carrying a lot emotionally and physically. At this point I was well into my pregnancy and now that all the "unpleasantries" were out of the way, I could completely focus on my unborn baby.

I woke up the next morning feeling like a super-hero. The night before I had slayed some of the most powerful dragons ever to convene in one family. Don't get me wrong, I took some painful gut punches and reality check slaps to the face, but ultimately I conquered a fear and removed my biggest obstacle. Everyone knew the truth now and there was no reason to hide or be ashamed. So, I went to work like normal and began making plans for my future. No more procrastination as I had a plate full of tasks to tackle. I was positive, focused, and motivated. My post 9/11 would be different and this was my Day 1.

THE GAME CHANGER

By: Michele Magaña

It started out as an ordinary summer Monday in our Virginia town, where I was a public high school French teacher. My husband of ten years and I were in the process of opening our very own company. We had a decent life together, a "tolerable" relationship. Love and commitment remained, but the pressures of raising three active sons, paying the bills and balancing the remaining time had begun to take its toll. The energy that anchored us had transitioned from passion and shared dreams to duty, responsibilities, and familiarity.

We were often too tired to treat one another with the thoughtfulness that filled our early years. Now clouds of unresolved bickering hung heavily in the air between us. We always blamed the other for our irritabilities and frustrations. In anger, we would threaten one another with abandonment. During the worst of those times we flung the word "divorce" about like an undetonated hand grenade.

Our friends and family assured us that our struggles were normal and all would be okay. We wanted to believe them, but inside I think we were both starting to wonder if we had made the right decision selecting each other some ten years ago. I'm not sure where we would be today had those thoughts been allowed to fester. But our thoughts changed, everything changed on that ordinary Monday when my phone displayed an unknown number.

The caller identified himself as a police detective. My heart froze. My boys were with me, but my husband wasn't. Was my sweetheart okay?

"Mrs. Magaña? Are you Mrs. Michele Magaña?" said the detective. His voice was cold. He informed me that he had my husband in custody. Before he could say anything else, I knew that the detective was mistaken. My husband was innocent. We had our problems, but he was a gentle person who always lived by the letter of the law.

I took slow, even breaths, determined to maintain my calm but inside my mind raced. Innocent or not, being a person of color in police custody was a dangerous situation that many did not survive.

"What are the charges?" I asked again. Again, the detective refused to tell me. He seemed to enjoy this game. The worst was not being able to hear my husband's voice to know if he was safe. The detective would not allow me to speak to him.

"My husband has the right to one phone call and I am respectfully requesting to speak to him," I said. I had once considered a career in law so I knew my rights.

"I'm calling on his behalf," the detective replied as if he was talking to a child. My blood surged hot up to my ears. This was not legal. The frustration I felt at that moment began to overtake me. My legs shook as I tried to keep my voice from trembling in fear and anger. I had to keep it together! My ability to communicate at this moment could determine the course of events for all of us forever.

I fought back my desire to threaten the detective over the phone. I feared he would retaliate against my husband behind the scenes. I didn't know if he was hurt or even alive.

I grabbed my three boys and we proceeded to the precinct. My mother offered to drive and I surrendered the wheel, my nerves were not up to the task. Once we arrived, we were informed that my love had been transported to a maximum-security prison. My mother, the boys and I were stunned! How could they transport him to prison without an arraignment, without a charge?

I soon realized I could not fight for my husband alone. I sought legal representation and the best attorney in the city. I needed someone who understood the plight of people of color and could adequately represent him. My mother taught the son of the best African American attorney in the city; We called him!

Returning from a trip, he agreed to meet us at the prison. He came straight from the airport and met us around 10:30 p.m. My mother and I drove to the prison where they were holding my husband. I don't remember much from that day, but I remember the darkness and the silence of the night. For such an evil place, the prison had a strangely majestic feeling. I wondered which space held my husband.

Was he ok? Was he even alive? Was he hurt? Searching for him in the darkness, I prayed for God's mercy and protection. I needed God and the *right* attorney. The lawyer greeted us at the entrance of the prison with a powerful handshake. I shook his hand all the while praying he could maneuver us out of this storm.

I surveyed the visiting area with shock and some sadness. Black families and poor whites made up a large proportion of the room's occupants. I couldn't help wondering if they could afford proper legal representation. I immediately felt blessed to have an attorney by my side.

I looked around the room at every woman and child. Were their loved ones innocent or guilty? My innocent husband was sent to a maximum-security prison in a matter of minutes. Were any of them facing similar circumstances? That night was a cruel reminder of the injustice we face in this country and our vulnerability at the hands of law enforcement based on the color of our skin.

I felt helpless and scared for my husband. All of the problems, issues and concerns I might have had about my marriage began to melt away. The thought that I might not ever see my husband again made me realize just how significant he was to my life. I thought of my boys, how his light showed up in each one of their faces, but in different ways. I thought of our life, our business, where we were headed in our next phase. My heart and body ached for him.

Upon arrival at my husband's prison block, we were told that he could only have one visitor. Although the boys and I desperately wanted to see him, I told our attorney to check on him. Before he walked through the doors, I told him my husband was *Hispanic*. I'm really not sure why I had held onto that fact.

The lawyer looked at me as if I had grown an additional head. He asked me if my husband was legal and if he had a criminal record. I assured him that my husband was a legal citizen, homeowner, husband, and loving father of three without a criminal record. The lawyer nodded. My anxiety only heightened as the doors closed behind him.

The boys absorbed the experience in disbelief. Their expressions reflected pain, but they remained quiet. I needed them to see the injustice of what they were witnessing and I wanted to teach them by example how to fight the system. The wait was cruel. Suddenly the lawyer returned. He shared the charges for the first time and our mouths dropped, incredulous. My sadness turned to anger and I vowed we would fight the police department to the end. The attorney said he would make my husband his priority and asked me to go home and sleep. I walked the attorney to his car, tears flowing down my cheeks. They were tears of determination.

I gripped his fingers tightly. "My family is in your hands," I told him. "My husband does not deserve this. He is innocent. The only just outcome will be his release."

Ever since I received that phone call, my heart starting beating so loudly I could almost hear it through my chest. Each breath came quick and shallow. I honestly believe my high blood pressure erupted that night. As my mother drove us to her house that evening, I only remember wanting to remain strong for the boys. Still quiet, they seemed to be evolving overnight. At my mom's house, the boys and I collapsed in one bed. I cuddled with them until they fell asleep. I later went to my mother's room where I cried uncontrollably. She hugged me and allowed me to take out my frustration and anger.

She then told me, "They pissed Mama off! We're going to fix their asses! They do not know who they are messing with!"

I remember waking up in the boys' bed. While they continued to sleep, I got up and fell to my knees. *"Dear God, please forgive me for all of my sins. I know I have worked very hard on my marriage very broadly, but I am neglecting my husband. If you will return him to me, I promise to love and cherish him with all my heart."*

My mind twisted around how we even got here. Had we become so consumed with the boys and the daily demands of life that we had begun to take each other for granted? Were we even still interested in or enthusiastic about each other anymore? Even though we had thrown about the word "divorce" in anger, we knew it was not an option. We loved each other, but we had become strangers in the night, roommates. Clearly, we needed a jolt.

Neither one of us was expecting something as terrifying as the threat of lifetime *incarceration to be the game- changer for our marriage.*

Months later, my husband revealed to me that he had also asked God for a second chance with me. He had vowed to love me more, to cherish me more and to be more present as my life partner, to be the husband that I deserved.

We had wished for the same thing on the same night.

The next day, we all went to his arraignment. Our world shattered once again when he came out with shackles on his wrists and legs.

"Why do they have Dad in chains, Mommy? He didn't do anything." All three boys looked at me, incredulous and their stare was very clear: "Fix this Mommy, Fix this!" Enraged, I promised the boys that Daddy will come home. I did not know when or how but as a parent I needed the boys to hold on to hope. *Hope is all we had!*

The next day I met with the lawyer and we added an investigator to our legal team. Our attorney worked tirelessly to free my husband. Two days later, he called me. "Go pick up your husband."

I was overjoyed. This ordeal had lasted only three days, but it felt like months. The police had arrested the wrong man and my husband would be home by the evening! The boys and I went to pick him up. The police did not even apologize for the trauma they had caused. "He's in good spirits," the officer said. I looked at him with disdain. *Good spirits*? I thought. What other type of *spirits* would they expect someone to be in after being falsely accused and sent to maximum security prison with all rights denied? The arrogance and the gall! This department will remember our name, I said to myself.

We proceeded to pick up my husband. As he walked up the hill, the boys ran to him. They hugged him and for the first time since this ordeal, all three broke down in tears. I allowed the boys to have their moment with their dad. I looked at him from afar and he looked at me. Our relationship felt different somehow, renewed! I saw him as if for the first time. He looked rejuvenated. I noticed every beautiful line in his face. His dark hair, his round face, his brown eyes. He looked handsome, beautiful. He was *My Husband.* I reveled in the moment.

At a restaurant later, my husband was quiet. "*America is a very dangerous place for blacks and Hispanics,*" he said. "*Because the white police officer could, he did! I can't believe I am still alive!*"

We settled into something close to normal. The thought of losing their Dad had seemed to rejuvenate the boys as well. They hovered around him. Sometimes they would hug him for no apparent reason.

One day while shopping at Sam's, we ran into one of the detectives from my husband's case. She was Hispanic. She was so glad to see my husband that she moved toward us quickly, smiling. She proceeded to tell him in Spanish that she knew that he was innocent all along. She kept telling the detective in charge that they *may* have the wrong man. However, her hands were tied as the detective who was handling the case had his mind made up.

That detective did not care whether or not my husband was innocent. He stated that my husband would be one less Hispanic to worry about. He had been scheduled for deportation that Friday. I was stunned and confused! How could a *legal* and *innocent* citizen be deported?

My husband's response never wavered, "He can so he did!" I interpreted that to mean that my husband felt the officers had too much control, especially the white ones.

The Hispanic detective was so glad that my husband was able to get legal representation and reunite with his family. "I am happy for you, not many Hispanics are as fortunate," she said.

I quickly asked her if she would be willing to share this information with our lawyer. We were appalled at the fact that the detective in charge could play with someone's life just because he could. She declined and stated that her family needs her income. She told us the police eventually apprehended the right perpetrator. He was indeed a Hispanic male. Our lawyer expunged my husband's record.

Over time my husband shared his experience that fateful day. He told me that it was God and his sons that kept him alive. I was scared at what he was about to share but kept quiet as he vented.

He told me six police cars and at least 20 police officers surrounded our house. The boys and I were at my mother's. Using our home as a makeshift torture chamber, they taunted him, pushed him and slammed him against things, trying to get a reaction out of him. While those officers physically abused him, another set of officers held onto their gun holsters in a menacing manner.

My husband is certain that they expected him to defend himself and if he did, they would shoot him and be justified in doing so. He could not believe the pain they inflicted upon him. "I wanted to defend myself!" he said. The thought of the boys being raised without him prevented him from reacting. The police would have called his shooting necessary because he was acting in a *violent* way.

My husband spoke, stunned at their hatred for Hispanics, "Their eyes exuded hate Michele, pure disdain for me! Their voices were cold and condescending! I don't know how blacks survive in the U.S. There is the written law and there is the white man's law. I am not supposed to be here, they wanted to kill me!"

My husband firmly believes that he is alive today because of God. He said the police wanted him to admit that his name was not his name. With his name they could not find any criminal history, no felonies, no misdemeanors, not even a speeding ticket. Surely he was using a fake name. He refused to comply. He only requested his phone call which was denied repeatedly.

Chills ran through my body! That he was alive and talking to me was a miracle. He could have died in custody, as many people of color do. It was God's plan for us to be here today talking about this. We hugged and it was understood that we were given another chance to get it right.

I read somewhere that the world's saltiest body of water is the Dead Sea. Everything that flows into the Dead Sea stays there, preventing anything from flourishing. Similarly, when a marriage has no outlet, it can risk becoming like the Dead Sea, lifeless. That's what had happened to us. The fear of losing each other forever changed the game. With the rebirth of our marriage came the renewal of the friendship we had also lost. We are now *our true friends*. Asked to be part of the marriage ministry at our church, we agreed and many were inspired by our story and our longevity. Because of what had happened to us and how we persevered, we can say we practice what we preach.

For example, I have always been an athlete. However, for the very first time, my husband joined my fitness journey and together we created our joint physical journey. Working out together benefits our health, both mentally and physically. Many elements of life can be stressful on a marriage. Our joint fitness journey is a huge stress reliever.

EVOLVE

We date once every two weeks. Our date nights provide another outlet. On our dates we can discuss our relationship, our needs and we check in on our feelings and gage our happiness. We look forward to dating and it keeps our marriage alive.

We recently celebrated our 20th wedding anniversary. I surprised my husband every month up to our wedding month with a romantic activity. *Celebrate your loved ones. Don't take your spouse for granted because, in the blink of an eye, he or she can be taken away from you. My husband was taken from me. I was very fortunate that God gave him back.*

We were granted a second chance and we choose to live our lives to the fullest every day! Should God call either one of us home, we will leave this earth knowing that we dedicated our lives to loving each other through God. That phone call will forever be *our game changer*. It evolved our marriage from being loving roommates to a powerhouse couple dedicated to their successful partnership.

THE MILITARY DID NOT BREAK US

By: Monica Busanet

My memories of that day are still very clear. As I stepped off the plane in Lawton, Oklahoma on a cold windy night in January, I had no idea what was in store for me. On that Sunday, January 2008, I had no idea that I would meet my soulmate just weeks later, or that we would create a child together and get married. I had no idea because at the time I just knew I was destined to be with the man I was dating when I stepped off that plane. Hello Oklahoma! I was ready to serve the next two and a half years of my military career at Fort Sill Army Base.

I arrived at Fort Sill after returning from Schweinfurt, Germany and a fifteen-month deployment in Iraq. My yet to be husband was also returning to Fort Sill after a fifteen-month deployment in Iraq as well. From the moment I saw him I thought to myself, who is this jokester trying his best to hit on me? Being me, I didn't give him the time of day. But something about him kept drawing me to him. Maybe it was his persistence, his swag, or his energy.

When I allowed that first conversation with him, it felt as if we were old friends from our school age days. We talked as if we had known each other for a lifetime. However, I pretended as if I didn't notice. I was determined to remain committed to my old relationship because I wanted it to work out. Months went by and we remained friends until the day came when my relationship ended. Although I didn't want the relationship to end, it had run its course. Some might say that my husband was my rebound guy and a relationship with him was not going to work, but there was something different about this man and our chemistry.

We started dating each other shortly after my old relationship was over. Dating was fun and he opened my eyes to so many new and different things. We would go on trips together, have lunch together, talk on the phone for hours, and just enjoy each other's company. The entire time we dated, I figured the relationship we were building would be short because he was due to leave Oklahoma for Fort Bragg, North Carolina. As a military woman, I knew nothing was going to become of what we had. He would go, I would finish my time in Oklahoma and move on to what was next for me.

I wasn't sure I even wanted what we had to last any longer. Deep down I just wanted to cherish the short, great time we had together and move on with my life. I was too young to make a commitment and not ready for anything more. The days flew by and June 2008 came quickly. The last night we spent together was sad, neither one of us wanted to part ways. We both knew that it would end, and we would likely never see each other again. We understood the life we lived and accepted that fact.

Fast forward two weeks later. I was not myself; my body didn't seem normal. I was more agitated than usual, and everything was off. My friend suggested I take a pregnancy test. So, I took it and was in disbelief with the results. I was pregnant by a man I had only known for a few months, a man I barely knew. Even though I knew our relationship was going to end, I couldn't deny the chemistry. Was I in love?

I immediately called him and told him about the baby. I was surprised and relieved when he said, "Everything will be okay, and we'll make this work. If you need anything let me know, it will be ok." That was good to hear, but there was no way we could be together because of our deployments. I went through the entire pregnancy alone, no father for my child and no family to lean on. It was hard but I got through it.

On February 2009 our beautiful baby boy was born. I couldn't have asked for a more perfect child. It was a joyous and sad day all in one. The day of our son's birth his father was serving yet another deployment in Iraq. I gave birth and he didn't even know. I waited for his call the next day and nothing came. Our son was two days old before his father knew he was born. I was blessed to have friends by my side, but the person I wanted there the most wasn't.

I went through the entire pregnancy and childbirth alone. Eventually he came home and immediately flew to Oklahoma to see us. During this time, we decided we would do what we had to do for our son to make sure he had a great life. Doing what we had to do didn't mean marriage to us at that time; it meant raising our son together and providing for him to ensure he had a wonderful fulfilled life even if we didn't marry.

On December 14th, 2009 we said our vows with our son in tow. There were no other loved ones by our side. We didn't need anyone else. We knew what we wanted and that was to be a happily married family. And that we were, at least that's what we thought.

Things were rough for our young marriage. I didn't get a chance to leave Oklahoma right away. Months passed by, and I was sad almost every day, the only thing that kept me sane was our son. Day in and day out I longed to be with my husband. I looked to my friends who were having babies and getting married and hated that I couldn't have what they had. I constantly wondered why me? How did I get so unlucky? I prayed and prayed for change and to be with my husband, I was desperate for it. Finally, August 2010 came, and I got reassigned to Fort Bragg, NC. Finally, we were going to be a family. Things were really looking up for us. We were happy but struggling to be one. We had never lived together, and we had never raised our son together.

My parenting style was different from his, and our upbringing and beliefs were different. So naturally we clashed. I believed that your child should have a voice in the family and have the ability to express how they feel. My husband didn't feel that way. He always felt that as the parent it did not matter what our child thought about a situation that directly affected him or how he felt about it. I didn't have that voice growing up, so I knew I wanted different things for my children. I wanted our children to have the ability to respectfully say how they felt and have an opinion in matters that concerned them.

When things finally seemed as if they were working themselves out, I got orders to deploy again. This time I was leaving for a year to serve in Afghanistan. Our world shattered! How were we ever going to make this marriage work if we're always going in two different directions? September 2011 came, and it was time to part ways again. As we stood in the airplane hangar with hundreds of other families and soldiers saying their last goodbyes, I fought hard to hold back my tears. I wasn't ready to leave my two-year-old son and I wasn't ready to leave my marriage again as we were finally blending as one. As I boarded the plane with tears in my eyes, I knew from that day forward something had to change.

Life was hard and all the back and forth between deployments and training was starting to weigh on our relationship. We were never going to know what it was like to really be married. Between deployments and trying to maintain a marriage thousands of miles away from one another it seemed nothing could go right. The worst came on June 1, 2012 when devastation struck the Forward Operating Base. I was on that base in Afghanistan. A one-thousand-pound Vehicle Borne Explosive Device was driven into the small forward operating base. Afghani Nationals swarmed our base in an attempt to hurt or even kill us. Several people were hurt; luckily none of us lost our lives that day. We were without hot meals, and basic needs for days/ weeks while we tried to get everything back into order. Life would never be the same anymore. I soon realized that life is short, and we only have one to live.

From that point forward I knew the military was no longer for me. I returned home one year later to my loving husband and son with a part of me still left in Afghanistan. I tried hard to rebuild a relationship with both my husband and son that I felt was damaged from being away. At this time in my life I made the difficult decision to let my military career go and focus on life as a wife and mom.

In January 2013, I said my final goodbye to the military. If my marriage was going to work and I was going to be the best person I could be for my family, I knew I had to give it up. Little did I know my husband was contemplating the same decision. He made the decision to leave the military without my input and in August 2013 he said his final goodbye to his military career as well. This was the beginning of something new for us, the beginning of our marriage in our eyes. Although we had been married for almost 4 years, we were still like newlyweds having barely spent two years together.

In June 2013, we rented our home to a beautiful family, packed up our truck with our

four-year-old son and dog and hit the road to travel more than 3000 miles across the country to begin our lives as military veterans. This is where our journey as a married couple began.

The sun was shining bright when we arrived in Rancho Cucamonga, Southern California. We wanted something different, a huge change of location. We were determined to enjoy every moment of this new journey. We had a plan and were going to stick to it. I planned to attend school and finish my bachelor's degree and my husband would be working for an oil refinery company with a military friend of his. Nothing could stop us, no more early mornings and late nights, no more deployments, and no more training that kept us apart for weeks at a time. We knew that what we had was a blessing. What we didn't know was the challenges that we would face.

We settled in our new place and while I was getting enrolled in school my husband was still trying to figure things out. The friend that we thought was going to help him with work ended up failing him and ultimately our family. My husband had to figure something out fast, so without hesitation he decided to go back to school. I didn't like the idea of him going to school because I knew he didn't enjoy school and wouldn't take it seriously. Although we always tried to work through the problems, we had together it seemed like there was always something. We found it difficult to agree on things and it would cause arguments between us. I hated having to waste money on school, but it seemed like we had no other options. We needed money and work was hard to come by in California. The lack of money became a big problem for us because we were so used to having money and saving to cover unexpected expenses.

The money we had managed to save was going fast. We argued about any and everything: money, our son, bills. Life was stressful but we kept moving forward. We just couldn't get back on the path we were on as a dually employed military couple. We wanted to keep living as we had been when we were in the military, but we didn't have the same income nor the same drive.

We kept at it with school and our plan was paying our bills and kept food on the table. Life was good but learning to work as a couple was hard. Time kept moving forward, we had to make a change. The change came in a different way than I expected it to come. I wanted another child. My husband wasn't on the same page with me, but I wanted the baby. A couple of weeks later we came to a verbal agreement to get pregnant despite everything that we were going through. We found out I was pregnant in February 2014. Although we wanted to believe that bringing another baby into the world would bring us back together as one, it didn't. My hormones got the best of me and I was even more agitated in our marriage. We both wanted out at several points in our marriage.

Our baby girl was born October 2014, strong and healthy. We decided at this point that we would do everything we could to make our marriage work. We knew that if we continued as we were going, our marriage wasn't going to last much longer. We had to learn to live our lives the best we knew how, outside of the military. There wasn't going to be any more time apart where we could just restart. We wanted this and now was the time to learn how to make it work. We had to learn to communicate with one another and let each other know how we're feeling. We had to learn how to compromise when it was necessary. We needed to know how to manage the money we had. Most of all we needed a new home away from California. We loved California but knew it wasn't meant for us to spend a lifetime. California was extremely expensive and in order to live comfortably we knew moving was our only option. We had nothing to lose by leaving California and everything to gain.

We spent less and saved the little money we had in a quest to move. We didn't know where we wanted to move so we picked the top three places: Virginia, North Carolina, and Georgia. We choose these places based on the job market, cost of living, and being closer to family. After months of going through the process of elimination, we decided on North Carolina. This move was going to be even harder than the last because financially we had to come up with all the money on our own and we didn't have the military to carry us through. The transition wasn't easy and there were many times where it seemed as if we weren't going to make it. Saving was even harder with a new baby at home. I was depressed and stressed many days and didn't know how we were going to make it. My husband ended up leaving school and getting a job as a trucker. This was a huge strain because it felt like we were back in the military again. He was on the road for weeks at a time and I was left back with the kids. I hated it. I was in school full time finishing my master's degree with two young children at home. With the extra money he was making we were finally able to save enough to move. We decided our new home would be Charlotte, North Carolina.

On May 2016, we said our final good-bye to our friends and the state of California. Our new journey began in Charlotte. We moved into our new place and things were looking up for us. My husband found a job right away. He worked long days and most weekends, so we didn't see him a lot. It was hard, but we stayed positive. I spent that first summer home while I prepared the kids for school and daycare. I searched relentlessly for work and nothing seemed to work out for me. No one seemed to want to hire a military veteran with a lot of education.

While our marriage seemed to be working, finding work after the military and college became a struggle for me. The lack of work became another issue for our family and school was starting back for our son. We fell into more financial issues. Money was tight and I needed work. I felt bad for my husband, but he couldn't see it. I was disappointed in myself because I knew he was doing everything he could to keep our family afloat. I finally found work as a housekeeper with the Department of Veterans Affairs. My plan was never to stay there, but to use the experience as a stepping-stone for other opportunities. I stayed in the housekeeping job for two months and landed a job with another part of the VA and eventually the job I obtained utilized my degree in Human Resources. With both of us now working life wasn't any easier, but we were able to keep going despite everything.

We got to a point in our relationship where we knew we needed to seek some type of therapy or counseling. The start of our relationship was very untraditional. We faced challenges, financial issues, parenting issues, and military issues. We needed to hear from someone else; a professional on how to fix our marriage. We both agreed that it would be the right thing to do. I found a good therapist and she helped us tremendously. After we deemed we had enough tools to keep our marriage loving and happy, we stopped going. We continued to use the tools she provided and kept moving forward. I joined her First Wives Club and learned that many women and relationships have highs and lows the way we did. The best thing I learned from the group is how to financially free us.

On January 2019, we made the decision to be financially free by the end of the year. We prayed about it, we believed it, we wanted it. We knew that in order to make it happen we had to take what money we had and start paying off our debt a little at a time. If we received extra money, we would use it to pay debt. We eventually were able to pay off all our credit cards, cars, student loans, and pay for a lavish vacation for our family. Next we were able to build our credit and we gained financial freedom by October 2019.

We had met our goal, so that same month we went into a contract to build our new home. Although the process was stressful, we came into February 2020 closing on our brand-new home. In April 2020, we were able to purchase two luxury cars of our dreams. We made it through so much but kept working at it. It was and is never easy for us. Life got in our way several times as it does for everyone, but because we were dedicated to marriage and wanted it to work, we did what we needed to do to keep our union strong.

After counseling and learning how to speak and care for each other we came out on top. My life is fulfilling now, not because of the material things we have, but because we now have a healthy marriage. Our story doesn't end here, we know that we will have more challenges come our way, but we know how to handle them now. With faith, I know we can overcome any new setback we may have. We evolved from a marriage with problems that seemed insurmountable, to a marriage where we received the tools to build a strong marriage able to overcome all obstacles. We are ever evolving; the military did not break us!

THEY SAVED ME

By: Shumon Spears Hudson

It had been a long week and I was exhausted mentally, spiritually and physically. I was lonely although I was a married woman. The smile on my face wasn't real and it was getting harder and harder to pretend I was happy. You see I had three young sons at the time. They were six months, two, and five years old. In that moment I floated outside of myself. I fed the boys, smiling and playing with them. Then I bathed them all with bubbles and toys in the tub. Finally, I settled them in front of the television with one of their favorite cartoons.

Carefully, I wrote a letter to my mom explaining that I'd had enough and that everyone would be best without me. I shared with her the secrets that I'd been holding in for so long and ended my letter with, "I love you, Dad, my brother and my boys. Please take care of them like I can't."

Up the stairs I went to run myself a hot bubble bath. I turned on the speaker in the bathroom with gospel music loud enough to drown out my sobs. I said a prayer to God asking him to forgive me and to please look after my family as I slowly began to sink down into the water. First to settle in was my shoulders, then my neck. I took a deep breath and slid down to my chin as I began to sob and tears rolled down my face uncontrollably. Next in was my ears as I tried to drown out the sounds around me that might keep me from doing this. I saw the water crest on the tip of my nose, closed my eyes and I dared myself to take my final breath. Before I could take that drastic step, I heard God say to me, "Get up! You know me better than this!" Gasping for air and spitting out water, I sat up and I cried in that same tub that was supposed to take my life until the water got cold. I heard someone knock on the door. "Mommy, my brother is crying, are you coming soon?" In that moment I knew I was all my sons had and I needed to fight for my life and theirs.

EVOLVE

You see, I grew up in a loving Christian home. My mom and dad took great care of me and my brother. We had a beautiful home, never went without anything that we needed and we had a family that loved us more than anything. As I grew older, I felt alienated by everyone around me. Junior High School is where this began. For some reason I didn't feel pretty like my friends. I was different, never truly fitting in with the "Popular" crowd.

I had my own set of friends and while many of them had friends in the "IN" crowd, I never felt good enough for them. I could place some of the blame on this girl who bullied me my seventh grade year. She made it a point to let everyone know that I was ugly and nobody liked me. Then she would glare at me any time our paths crossed. I hated Junior High School. While all of the girls were gaining boyfriends, I gained loneliness. I didn't quite trust my small group of friends to share with them what I was feeling. They wouldn't understand, they were liked by many. And I definitely wasn't going to share my problems with my mom. I just felt like she wouldn't understand what I was going through, and would suggest for me to do things that would alienate me even more. I wanted a boyfriend like my friends. Someone to talk to, hold hands with, talk on the phone all night with. By my ninth grade year my dream came true. A young man took the time to get to know me and he made me feel beautiful. He cared about my feelings when I felt no one around me understood. I still remember him; he was a vital part of my growth. The memories would be the foundation for the love I sought as an adult.

High School was such a struggle. I didn't go to Junior High School with the neighborhood kids, my parents sent me to a Lottery School that was supposed to offer better instruction and a better environment. Then to make matters worse, my family moved to a new neighborhood where I didn't know anyone. I was miserable and I made it a point to let my parents know. At the time our new neighborhood didn't consist of many people that looked like me and I never went outside unless it was to get in the car to leave. I didn't realize then how blessed I was we moved to a better place.

My first year of high school was so awkward. It was tough making new friends, trying to determine where I fit in and creating my own style in clothes, hair, and make-up. Once again, I just didn't fit in. To make matters worse, I had strict rules at home and I wasn't allowed to do what so many others were allowed to do such as hanging out and dressing a certain way. While other girls were noticed by boys and being called beautiful, I can count on one hand how many times I heard those words in high school.

I felt like the ugly duckling. I tried out and made the letter girl squad and that is where my transformation began. I was finally spending time with a group of popular girls and this brought on a new life for me. I was invited to parties, was allowed to accept rides in their cars to hang out after basketball games, and so many other things. I gained my first high school boyfriend my Junior Year and he also understood how different I was. I had someone to talk to and share my dreams and goals with, but never trusted him with my insecurities. Nobody knew how fearful I was of being judged or that my new boyfriend would leave because I didn't add up to the other girls. At that time I felt that he was all I had to make me feel golden.

Fast forward to my college days. I stayed local in Charlotte, NC. Many times I wonder what my life would have been like if I'd gone away to college. If I knew then what I know now; I would have made much different choices. But I knew God had a plan for me. The good news was that my best friend and I since first grade both went to UNC-Charlotte. We were back together again and I was sooo happy! Walking the campus of UNC-Charlotte we were inseparable, lots of laughs, parties in the student center and boys, boys, boys. I'm not sure where this new confidence came from but I was loving it.

It was Friday night and it was time for some fun. Fresh box braids up in a bun, my skin, smooth as brown sugar, my body tight and stacked like a sassy stallion rocking Daisy Dukes and a crop top. Lips glistening from gloss so thick and shiny you could see your reflection in them. We pull up in the parking lot and it was so crowded that our excitement grew as we walked toward the door. The Sugar Shack had ladies and men alike all over the place waiting to get in as "Mr. Boombastick" played with thick bass from the speakers inside filling my body with electricity, ready to hit the dance floor with the latest moves.

Inside I could feel myself being sized up from every man that I walked by. Smiles and grabs of the hand, and let me buy you a drink followed. Hmmm, I smiled inside, thinking the night is still young. I danced until the material on my outfit was drenched with sweat so thick I felt the weight of an extra five pounds. Finally the last song of the evening played and as I headed for the door, I heard, "Lets' Dance!" "Sure!" I say.

EVOLVE

He pulled my body toward his and I could feel the strength of every strong muscle in his body. "I want to be your man, I want to be your man," the song blared. Lost in another world and moving in rhythm to the words of this song, our exhilarated and sweaty bodies moved as if one. In that moment there was a certain desire that I could not describe. I felt wanted, I felt safe, I just felt. This one chance meeting led to years of dating this somewhat younger man who was two years my junior. We married at the tender age of 23 and 21. What was I thinking? I was ready but was he? We had a child together, we moved in together, marriage was the next step right? I knew then that we loved each other but I ignored the fact that we were unequally yoked by more than just our ages. The years after proved just how much.

One issue with us was that I am a big family person and his family wasn't as close knit. He never kept me from going to spend time with my family but so many times I went alone. He was a great husband in the beginning. He was a provider, a great father and he treated me like gold. We were involved in the church and our family had grown to include two more sons. I just knew I had the perfect life. Was I that naive to believe that we had the perfect relationship?

Something changed. I'm not exactly sure when or why. Suddenly he didn't look at me the same way with love and desire in his eyes. When we talked his words cut like a sword to my flesh. Why was he talking to me that way? From day to day there was a different reason for an argument. I usually kept quiet, holding everything in to keep the peace. I hated to argue.

Where did it go wrong? I worked, cooked, cleaned, was a good mother and an even better wife. Why wasn't I good enough for him? The compliments he once gave had turned to complaints. Now everything about me was wrong. How I wore my hair, how I dressed, who I spent time with. This began to impact how I felt about myself. Who was I becoming? How did I get here?

All I wanted to do was please him and to have a happy marriage and family. That wasn't good enough! Nothing was ever good enough! Soon he started coming home later and later. The calls slowed to a stop, the time we spent together came to a halt and the intimacy was non-existent. I was married and I was lonely. Those words don't belong together in the same sentence.

I knew something was going on, but I couldn't put my finger on it. I had small children so I couldn't let on that something was wrong. They could feel and see my every emotion so I hid everything that I was feeling for the sake of my children. In the garage I would go to scream, cry, pray, and punch things only to clean my face and hide it from my kids and from him. I began to get messages from people saying they saw him out with someone, and the messages continued to flood in.

The final message that told me my husband was at the beach with another woman hurt me to my core. God, why are you allowing me to hurt this way? My heart was crushed to dust. I didn't trust God at that moment to care for my heart. I didn't know what to think, what to say, how to feel? REALLY?! I am working my fingers to the bone, taking care of our home and you are out taking care of another home? To add to my pain I learned this woman was one who I worshipped God with, sang on the choir with, who ate dinner at my kitchen table, is now with my husband? How dare they make a fool of me!

I held on to the marriage. I told myself I was staying for my children because I wanted them to grow up with both parents in the home. So I continued to endure the heartbreak and the disrespect, thinking I was protecting my children. I didn't realize how staying likely hurt them more than it helped and in the process, my pain grew even larger than the lie that was my marriage.

We were approaching Christmas, one of my favorite times of the year. A time when spirits are light and the air is filled with excitement and joy. There was no joy for me, although I forced a smile for my children day after day. On Christmas Eve 2002, he didn't come home to help play Santa for our children and I knew I'd had enough. Through tears, I pulled out, set up, and put together toys for my children to be excited and happy the next morning. I wanted to throttle him when he walked in the door the next morning like nothing happened. Who is he? Why was he doing this? More importantly, why am I allowing him to treat me this way? Why didn't I love myself enough to walk away?

A few weeks later, I could no longer take the embarrassment. I felt confused, hurt, and caged in with no other way out. So I fed and bathed my precious gifts from God, wrote a note for my mom and ran the water in the tub. I cried as I began preparing to leave this earth in hopes that there would be someone better equipped for my children than me. But my attempt to end my life was quickly interrupted by God when I heard his voice clearly say to me, "Get up! You know me better than that!" God saved me!

EVOLVE

After I gained the strength to get up from the tub and get myself together, I went to check on my children and put everyone to bed and then I prayed. Every morning God dropped scriptures in my spirit to give me enough strength for that day. I began to make preparations to leave my husband. I had to have somewhere we could go and feel safe, to create a loving environment for my 3 young kings. I found a neighborhood and began the process of having a home built. Each moment of progress I felt closer to freedom. The lot was cleared, the foundation poured, the walls and roof complete. No one knew what was going on. The closer we got to freedom, the shorter our conversations became and I knew he could tell something was going on.

He wanted to leave and I didn't stop him. I changed the locks on the doors only for him to bust the door in when I wasn't home available for him to come at his leisure to get more of his things. With a broken door he left us exposed, unsafe and he didn't seem to care. Again I felt empty, how could someone who claimed to love us treat us so bad?

The day came where I could pick up the keys to our new home. I had been slowly packing and putting boxes in the garage for a few months now. I packed the remainder of our things while the boys were at school and I left. I left all of the heartache, feelings of uselessness, moments of insanity, mental anguish, and embarrassment in that home when I locked the door and walked away.

Even though I finally felt like I had a sense of peace in my life, I was still embarrassed that my marriage had failed. I hadn't yet healed from all of the hurt. So when he told me that he loved me and that he wanted our family back, I allowed him to move into the home, the safe haven that I had built for me and my children. Stupid me! I wanted my boys to grow up with both parents and I let him back in.

What was I doing? I allowed moments of insanity, insatiable lovemaking, and blind romance to draw me back into a relationship with someone who had shown me by his actions that he didn't want me. How could I be so blind, so dumb to think that he had changed so quickly. I just wanted to be loved and give love. He used my fragile heart as an opportunity to get back in to continue to control me. His attention to detail and care was so short lived. He was back to his old tricks, back to her and the worst part was I learned that she lived even closer to where I currently lived.

EVOLVE

The fight began when I actually caught him cheating and told him to decide. I was done with the lies, the embarrassment, with being mistreated. I just wanted to be at peace. "You don't get to control me any longer. It's either me or her and you damn sure can't have both," I told him. I headed down the stairs walking away from the loud argument he started when he pushed me. My oldest son was still awake, crying as he heard us arguing like the strangers we had become and me falling down the steps. He screamed, "Mommy, Mommy, stop, Mommy!" In response, I screamed up to my son to call the police NOW! I tumbled down 14 steps and a landing, ending at the bottom of the steps with my face 1 inch away from hitting the wall.

I thought I was going to die. I didn't know what else he would try to do to me. I was going to fight for my kids, so I got up and I fought him as much as I could. Throwing at him anything that I could get my hands on. Before the police, my parents, and my brother could get there he was gone. The police located him and told him to never walk through the doors of my home again.

How did my life get to this? This was not the woman I was raised to be. That horrifying moment changed everything for me. Nothing would keep me from being the best for my kids. Not even their father. My evolution began. The love for my sons SAVED ME!

In 2008, filing for divorce was one of the easiest and most difficult things for me to do. I took my vows seriously and ending it felt to me that I was disappointing God. But God made it very clear to me that I was making the best decision for all of us. I spent more time with my children, rebuilding our relationship, confirming for them that I would ALWAYS be there for them and that they had nothing to fear. We would be alright. My sons are my pride and joy, I will do anything for their happiness… I took the time to know, understand, and love the woman that I had become. I am wonderfully and fearfully made. I had to believe that, live that and breathe that!

Once my self-confidence grew, things began to change for the better. I had to remove the dead weight of my broken relationship. Almost immediately I began to feel better and be better. I walked away from a job that was causing me daily stress that I would bring home to my children. They didn't deserve this version of me. At the time I was not getting child support so I sold every piece of furniture in my home except our beds just to pay the mortgage and put food on my table. I didn't care; I just needed us to be ok. I could have easily gone to my parents for help but this was my battle, my fight, I had to earn the trophy for this one.

Soon career opportunities opened up that created even more opportunities to be the best for my boys. One step at a time; things improved. Even my social life began to gain some vibrancy as I took control of what made me happy and split that time with being a mom. I finally gained the strength to go out on my own if I wanted. I didn't need to be with anyone else, I was comfortable in my own skin. I was dating and life was good for me and my little family.

In March 2010, while I was living my best life, I met the man that would show me a love that I never knew existed. Godly love, Agape love, Intense love, and this same love flowed to my children. You see, I fell in love with the "Maintenance Man."

We met at a friend and neighbors home as he was completing some home improvement projects for her. She knew that I was looking for someone to lay hardwood floors, do some painting, etc. So one evening after work, she asked me over. After much procrastination and many excuses, I finally went and there was a handsome sight over her sink hanging a light fixture.

His smile like butter on a hot biscuit melted me where I stood. His strong arms extended displaying a well-toned physique. He smiled at me and I back at him. Then I realized OMG! Why didn't I fix my hair, remove the glasses, and put on some lipstick or something? All of these things flowed through my head. But he seemed to be pleased with the vision I presented that night. I was just simply me; no extras.

We exchanged numbers with a promise that he would come by to look at my project and provide a quote. Not long after the work on my projects began we became friends while the work was being completed. My boys had a different level of comfort around him that made me smile. He would talk to them and ask about their day, talk sports, and just have guy talk. He was always asking about my day, my school work. Was it small talk or was he flirting with me?

After all of the work was completed on my home, he asked me out on a date. The business relationship had now turned personal. It was one of the best dates I'd been on in a very long time. The conversation was thought provoking and exciting. Topics ranged from music to politics to love? He was chivalrous; he opened doors, pulled out chairs and always wanted to hold my hand. Oh my, did he come from a fairy tale?

He sent me flowers on the regular and checked on me and the boys on a daily basis. He helped with homework and cooking without my having to ask. Who was this person? I thanked God for bringing me this glimpse of what relationship happiness could be. Such a breath of fresh air! Not long after we met we claimed ourselves as exclusive and the fireworks haven't stopped.

In April 2011 he asked me to be his wife. I'll be honest, I was afraid after the first failed marriage. I told him I wasn't sure if I wanted to get married again.

"Can't we just be BFL's I asked?"

He said, "What is that?"

I responded, "Boo's for Life," and laughed.

He didn't find that amusing and said to me that if I wasn't interested in marriage then we should just call it quits and not waste each other's time. My eyes grew big as half dollars! Did he give me an ultimatum? Oh my! Marriage is a serious thing for me and not something that I take lightly so I had to be sure of my decision.

When I saw the love and care in his eyes not only for me but for my boys, I knew he was truly the one.

I never thought I'd feel this level of love again in my life. I had given up on love so many years ago. In those very moments my now husband saved me from myself. He took the time to chisel away every single brick that I'd put in place to protect my heart. He makes me feel like the most beautiful girl in any room that I am in. His smile makes me blush and the care in his voice makes me melt. His touch? Oh, his touch sends chills from the top of my head to the soles of my feet. His love for God, makes me love him even more. His soul mission is to make me happy and to protect and provide for our blended family. He's driven, kind, caring, Godly, and most of all; he's mine.

I never knew a love like this could exist. We are far from perfect but we are perfect for one another. He is the peanut butter to my jelly, the sugar to my Kool-Aid. I've evolved from a scared, forgettable young girl to a strong, confident, beautiful, unforgettable, no-nonsense woman. Look what happens when you wait on God. You evolve and you heal!

LOVING AN ADDICT

By: Deleisha L. Webb

I was molested by my uncle," I said very nonchalantly. This disclosure came out unexpectedly. We were sitting at a high top table at a sports bar. The music was so loud that it was hard to talk over the songs.

My friend looked up at me with tears in her eyes. "What do you mean you were molested by your uncle? Who Leisha? When? Did you tell your parents?" As my friend looked at me in shock and tears rolled down her cheeks, I checked out. I couldn't believe I had just disclosed that information. I had never told anyone outside of my family that I was molested when I was a little girl. As my friend and I sat and drank, the tears continued to flow. She cried. I hid my tears. Nevertheless, he saw us.

I saw him coming to the table. He looked concerned. He walked up to our table and said, "Is she ok? Do you all need something?" My first reaction was to look down at his hands. They were ashy. I took my lotion out of my purse and began to rub it on his hands. By the end of the night, I had given him my phone number. And so my story begins.

I was new to Charlotte by way of Kentucky. I moved to Charlotte in July 2005 and I met my ex-husband in March 2006. We met on a Saturday night. We had our first date on that Monday. Tuesday he came to my house and never left. Sounds crazy, right? From that day on, we were together every day and night. The only exception was when I went to Kentucky or when he went to his hometown of Laurinburg. Although we were inseparable, we did not spend a lot of time together. He was working three jobs. He was often busy working day and night. I remember when he confessed that he wanted us to be committed and work on a relationship. I told him that day "You don't have time for me." Little did I know that I would repeat that same statement several times over the next eleven years.

EVOLVE

Year after year after year, I made that same statement. Yet, I married him to have a companion. Doesn't make sense or does it? I wanted a partner to enjoy life with. I wanted to have someone that I could count on to enjoy dinner, movies or bowling. I wanted to have someone to walk through the park or around the lake. I wanted a partner to spend quality time with and connect intimately, emotionally and mentally. I wanted a partner to travel and explore the world with.

As I reflect on why I got married, I often wonder why I married for companionship and not for love. Yes, you read it correctly. I married for companionship. Did I love my husband? Absolutely! However, love was not the underlying reason I accepted his marriage proposal. Being a girl who never dreamt of getting married, I was not sold on a fantasy of love and happily ever after. I always felt that love is important and vital in a relationship but not the sole reason for marriage.

So why did I marry my ex-husband? I was a single mother of a 10-year-old when I met him. I was college educated with a few degrees. I had worked in state government since I finished my undergraduate degree in 1997. I had been on my own since I was 19. I was a strong woman. I was independent. I took care of myself and my son with little to no help from his father. However, I was tired of doing it alone. I often wondered what it felt like to be able to "just be" instead of being all. I wanted a companion. I wanted someone who I could depend on "if" I needed him. Therefore, I married him to have a companion. We married on April 4 2009.

For many years, my marriage was great! The newlywed years, as they call them, were refreshing and exciting! As the years passed by and we became empty nesters, things began to change. I quickly realized that the one thing that I married for, "companionship," was the one thing that I felt was lacking from my marriage. Yes, my husband loved me, cared for me, provided for me and desired me. Nevertheless, I did not have what I wanted or needed, his time.

My husband was addicted to work. I did not recognize it as an addiction early on in our relationship. The non-stop working was already spinning when I met him. At that time, he was working three jobs. As our relationship started to grow and he wanted a commitment, I told him that he did not have time for a commitment. He initially thought I was joking. I pointed out to him that he was too busy to develop a real relationship with me or anyone else. Over time, when I would make that comment, he would say, "I'll make time." That response became a running record in our home. However, I gave it the benefit of the doubt and assumed that things would change. Three years later, we got married. Things still had not changed. Between my full-time job and his full-time job plus two part-time jobs, we hardly spent any "quality time" together.

For the first year, our time together was limited. We had two boys that were very busy with sports – football, basketball, baseball, and track. Because I was so busy with the boys, I did not focus on the fact that my husband was working all the time. I sucked it up. I rationalized him working all the time by thinking that I did not have time for him either. His work schedule eventually became a problem in terms of him attending the boys' sporting events. I would be angry that he did not make the sacrifice to be at the games as opposed to working. Again, I rationalized it by thinking that we needed the extra money to take care of the boys and pay for all of their extracurricular expenses. I sucked it up.

By 2014, both boys graduated and moved out of the house. That is when my eyes opened up to the Empty Nest Syndrome – it is very real! The feeling of loneliness that took over me was unexplainable. I knew that the boys kept me busy. My son has played sports since he was 4 years old. It started with t-ball, then baseball, then basketball, then football and track – it was year-round sports so I was used to being busy. Honestly, my son's schedule is what gave me life. I did manage to get some time in there because I started traveling when he was very young. However, the majority of my time was spent traveling for my son's sports. When my bonus son came into my life, the rest of my time went to him. He also played sports and was sometimes on a different team than my son.

Being an empty nester, I no longer spent all of my extra time at sporting events. I simply had "extra time." It was during this time that I realized how much time I spent alone. I realized how much my husband was away from home. By this time, he was working his full-time job, doing security Thursday-Sunday evenings and doing other odd jobs – detailing cars, moving people, etc. He eventually bought a party bus too. My husband was what I called a "legal hustler." He did a little bit of everything to make money. It was as if he couldn't sit still. If he ever had any free time, he would make up some work to do. Security brought him home in the wee hours of the night. I went to bed alone. I woke up alone. I was always ALONE. ALONE. It hit me like a brick. Damn Deleisha, you are always by yourself. You are always ALONE.

When I say I went to bed by myself and woke up by myself, I do not mean that he stayed out all night. He never did that. My husband always came home. He just did not require much sleep. He would get home around 3 a.m. after working security at the club and he would be back up and moving by 7 a.m. No, he did not have a job that required him to be at work by 7 a.m. He would get up and detail cars or help someone move or go look for work.

My husband was never home. I began to feel empty. That feeling caused me to become insecure in my marriage. I started to wonder if he was out cheating on me and not working. I started to wonder if maybe he was seeing a woman at the club where he worked. As months turned to years, those questions began to consume me. When he was gone, I could not stop wondering if he was with other women. Insecurity overtook me. I began to question myself as his wife, was he sexually satisfied? Was I not paying him enough attention? Was I nagging him too much about staying home? Is he no longer attracted to me? Once the insecurities started, they became a rolling ball that never ended. Like a snowball, my insecurities grew from the size of a tennis ball to the size of a basketball. My once very secure, strong and confident persona quickly diminished.

Did I address it? Absolutely. Month after month. Year after year. I expressed my feelings of loneliness to my husband. I can remember crying to him. Begging him to stay home and not go to work some nights. Every year for our anniversary, we took a trip. During that trip, we would talk about how we could improve our marriage. We talked about what we needed or wanted more of from each other. I always expressed that I felt alone and lonely. I always asked him to work on balance between work and home. He would make some provisions. The provisions would last for a week or two and then he would fall right back in his routine of constantly working.

I asked him to go to counseling. First, he agreed. I made appointments for us and he would come up with an excuse about why he could not make it. Eventually, he flat out said he wouldn't go to counseling. I finally accepted the fact that my husband was a workaholic.

I looked it up on Wikipedia: Workaholic. "A workaholic is a person who works **compulsively**. The person works at the cost of their sleep, meeting friends or family. While the term generally implies that the person enjoys their work, it can also alternately imply that they **simply feel compelled** to do it. There is no generally accepted medical definition of such a condition, although some forms of stress, impulse control disorder, obsessive-compulsive personality disorder, and obsessive-compulsive disorder can be work-related. Much like alcoholism as a form of an alcoholic but in terms of work therefore a workaholic."

As I read the definition of a workaholic, there is one word that repeatedly shouts out to me. **Compulsively.** My husband worked at the cost of his sleep and his family. He has worked more than one job since the day I met him. Even when he wasn't officially "at work," he was still working. He would detail cars. He would help people move. He would help other people do their work. I have been asking my husband to make time for me since we got married. I have repeatedly asked, no begged him to make time for me. I can remember all of the times that I'd sit him down to discuss my concerns. I would express to him that I need him. I would tell him that I need my husband home with me. I expressed my disappointment about him missing the boys' sporting events because he was working. Football, basketball, baseball. He missed many games over the years because he was "working." I didn't expect him to stop working altogether. What I expected was that he would balance work and home. My husband did not have to work all the time to make ends meet. He had me. I was his wife. We were supposed to be a team. My husband **simply felt compelled** to work all the time. He has explained to me that work is all he knows. He has explained that he has worked his entire life and no one has ever given him anything.

Just like any other addiction, the effect on our marriage was devastating. Neglect. I felt like my husband neglected my needs – emotionally, mentally and physically. It was hard for us to maintain an emotional connection because we did not spend quality time together. Our time together was hit or miss. The mental connection was lacking because we lost the emotional connection. The physical connection was never an issue but that's all it was. Physical Sex. After years of feeling neglected and unwanted by my husband, I checked out. I no longer felt any connection with him.

How did I cope?

I threw myself into taking vacations. I took vacations out of the country. I took beach trips. I took road trips. I took trips across the country. I jumped on board with anything that gave me some attention and time. My husband never said a word. He never told me not to go. He never told me that we did not have the money to go. He never acted or appeared to be upset or angry over me leaving. His acceptance or lack of emotion about me constantly being on the go just added to my insecurities. In my mind, I felt like he wanted me to leave so he did not have to hear me complain about him always working. There were times when I felt like he wanted me gone so he could be with other women.

Today I do not believe that to be true. I do not believe that he had other women that he was entertaining. I can remember New Year's Eve about two years before we separated. We were eating at my favorite restaurant, On the Border. I wanted us to have a serious talk about my feelings. I said to him "I'm not going into 2016 like this with you. I will not be lonely in our marriage for another year." I was angry and hurt when I said this to him. I wanted him to understand me and tell me everything was going to be ok. I wanted so badly for him to tell me that he would make the changes and spend more time at home.

Instead, my husband started crying and he talked about how hard he worked to provide for our family. He was saying that he wanted me to be able to take vacations and go shopping. He told me that he wanted me to have everything that I wanted. He continued to cry as he told me that sometimes he would be hurting so badly from his back injury, but he still went to work for me. For us. For our family. As I listened to my husband explain his reasoning for working ALL the time and I watched him cry, I felt bad. I felt so sorry that he felt like he had to work even in pain just to provide for our family.

However, I also felt like he was not listening to me at that moment and he did not understand my feelings. By this time, year seven of our marriage, I had told him several times that I would rather have him at home with me than to have his money. I had told my husband that "we" are a team and where he lacked financially, I could step in. I made a decent salary. I could pick up the difference and I wanted to pick up the difference. That would mean that my husband could cut back on his hours and spend more time at home. I craved his attention and his time. I craved intimacy with him. I craved to be fulfilled mentally, emotionally and physically. By physical, I do not mean sex. Sex was never an issue in our marriage. Sex was the one thing he always made time for.

The Final Straw

I was preparing to leave for a 12-day vacation in California with a girlfriend. Our flight was leaving at 8:30 the following morning. The day before I left, my husband and I had spent the day with family. We enjoyed quality time with family and friends. We cooked hamburgers, ribs, steak and hot dogs on the grill. We listened to music. We talked. We laughed. The day felt so perfect. The sun was shining bright and the temperature was in the lower 80's. As we drove back to our house, I felt emotional and excited because I was going to spend the rest of the evening with my husband before leaving for vacation. That feeling was short-lived. His phone rang and he answered. This is all I heard "I'm headed home now. I just need to change and I'll be there. Immediately my eyes stung with tears. I could not believe I'd just heard my husband say he was going to work the night before my 12-day trip. I looked at him and asked if he was going to work. He looked at me and did not answer. I knew he didn't respond because he didn't want the argument. However, his lack of response was enough for me. The next morning, he drove me to the airport. We hugged. We kissed. I enjoyed California for the next 12 days.

Day 12 8:45pm. As my flight landed, my stomach was a ball of excitement. After being away from my husband for 12 days, I could not wait to see him. I missed him. I missed his touch. I missed his smile. I missed his laugh. All I wanted to do was to fall into his arms. Sure, we talked every day I was gone, but I missed his physical presence so much. I had even forgotten the pain felt before I left. My husband picked me up and greeted me with a BIG hug and kiss. We get in the car and head home. Before we were off the airport property, his phone rings. He answers, "Yes I'm coming. I just picked my wife up from the airport. I'll be there after I take her home. I have two other guys coming to work as well."

I felt like I had been sucker-punched in my chest. I remember thinking this has to be a joke. I looked at him waiting for him to say I didn't hear what I'd just heard him say. Immediately my eyes stung with tears. When he didn't respond, the tears fell. My entire body felt a pain that I didn't recognize. My heart hurt. My stomach hurt. My head hurt. I could no longer control my emotions. I begin to cry uncontrollably. All I thought about was my husband doesn't love me. He doesn't want me. He does not want this marriage. That day, at that time, I knew I could no longer continue to be second in his life.

We separated the following month. One year later, we divorced.

Evolved.

December 2019 – I chose Deleisha. For the last two years, I didn't feel like I had evolved. I didn't feel like I had healed. I felt like a failure because my marriage ended in divorce. Then I had an "affair" with my ex-husband. From March 2019-October 2019, I allowed myself to become involved physically with him. Because my heart had not healed, I easily and comfortably fell in place being with him. I was so angry with myself for giving myself to him for those 7 months. During that time, I realized that being with him brought back those same feelings of insecurity and loneliness. It took me falling into a state of depression for me to realize that I deserved something better from him or any other man.

When I think about it, I feel like that brief "affair" was a necessary process that helped me to evolve and heal. Today, I feel confident that I no longer romantically want my ex-husband. I no longer long for his attention. I no longer wait for his phone calls. I choose Me. I recognize that I am deserving of a man's complete love. I was worthy of his complete attention, his, complete commitment to me and our relationship. Because I have evolved, I will not allow myself to be in a relationship where I feel lonely, ashamed, embarrassed or unworthy of love.

I started my story disclosing that I was sexually abused as a child. What I learned from that experience was not to trust anyone to love me. I learned that I needed to guard my heart so that no one could hurt me again. My abuser is a family member. He should have protected me not hurt me. I trusted him. I loved him. I trusted those around me to protect me. That did not happen. As I transitioned into adulthood, I did not allow myself to open up and be vulnerable with anyone. The easiest way for me to avoid being vulnerable was to keep love out of my commitment and marry for companionship. Companionship gave me what I "thought" I wanted in my marriage. But it didn't give me what I ultimately "needed" in my marriage. My childhood trauma taught me two things: 1) I want to feel loved completely and unconditionally and 2) Don't trust anyone to protect and love me. Yes, they are a contradiction of each other.

Today, through the process of evolving, I have learned two things: 1) I want to feel loved completely and unconditionally and 2) In order to feel unconditional love, I have to be vulnerable and trust that my mate will protect and love me unconditionally. Sexual abuse is just one of my childhood traumas that has impacted my life. Combine that with the effects of growing up with a drug addicted parent and you have the raw, uncut version of Deleisha. One day, I will share the details of my childhood and adulthood traumas. For now, I'm working on me and my healing. I'm working on my evolution.

RESOURCES

National Domestic Violence - www.TheHotline.org

National Mental Health Network – www.PsychologyToday.com

Infertility Challenges - www.Gateway-Women.com

National Substance Abuse line - www.Samhsa.gov

Relationship Services – www.ItTakes2MarriageCoaching.com

ABOUT THE AUTHORS

April Taylor

Born and raised in South Carolina, April Taylor is the youngest of three siblings. She is the wife of Timothy Taylor, and they have three children. April co-founded Marriage Beyond Ministry, a non- profit organization in 2018. She is a Certified Life Coach and the owner of Becoming A Better You LLC.

"For I know the thoughts that I think toward you, saith the Lord, thoughts of peace, and not of evil, to give you an expected end." - Jeremiah 29:11(KJV)

Janet L. Jacobs

Janet L. Jacobs lives in Charlotte, NC. She has over 30 years of experience in Office Administration Services with an executive level of support in the fields of Engineering, EH&S, Facilities Management, Legal (insurance, legal services, and bar exam prep), and Pharmaceutical Leadership Development/Sales Training. She currently works for an elite North American climate control company in Charlotte.

She is a proud Mother; she singlehandedly raised three Daughters and one Son, all successful in their own right. She is a devoted wife to her husband of six years. They enjoy life together as empty nesters.

Janet enjoys cooking for family and friends, reading, gardening, knitting/crocheting, singing, bargain shopping, and spending time with her family.

Connect with Janet online:

Email: Janetbethea4@gmail.com

Facebook: https://www.facebook.com/janet.mableton

Instagram:https://www.instagram.com/artshoneybunny

Twitter: https://www.twitter.com/janetljacobs4

Shania Elliott-McDowell

Shania Elliott-McDowell is a wife and a mother of four. She was born and raised in Brooklyn, NY, and now lives in Charlotte, N.C. She proudly served two years in The United States Army and eight years in The National Guard. Shania has attended Johnson & Wales University, where she obtained her Associates in Culinary Arts. She is the proud owner and Chef of Decadent Chefs. She has also played football with the Carolina Queens Women's football team. Shania is the founder of the upcoming nonprofit organization called Happiness Is Vibrant. She is currently working on her next writing project, and her forthcoming anthology will be out later this year. Her hobbies, being a mom, are reading, writing poetry, and creating new dishes. Her favorite quote is by Maya Angelou "If you are always trying to be normal, you will never know how amazing you can be."

Michelle W. Pennington

Michelle (Chelle) Pennington is a native of Cleveland, Ohio, who now resides in the Queen City, Charlotte, NC. After moving with her husband and five children, she vowed to make the most of her new environment and try all sorts of new endeavors, one of them is changing her career path. A life-long sales executive and marketer extraordinaire, Michelle decided to take a leap of faith and become an entrepreneur – creating and managing her successful photo booth company, The Photo Booth Lady. Having accomplished the unthinkable, it was time for the next challenge, becoming a best-selling author. This book is Chelle's debut contribution to the literary world. It is a heartfelt and brutally honest depiction of a challenging time in her life, including the many ebbs and flows she experienced. Evolve: From Heart Break to Hearts Healed is Chelle's perfect introduction to all readers – ENJOY!

Michele Magaña

Michele Magaña was born in Washington, DC. Her father is from Cameroon in West Africa and her mother is from Washington DC. She is an educator and a business owner. She lived all over the world and she is a globetrotter.

Her chapter details the raw reality of police brutality and racial profiling in America. Despite the challenges and pain her family endured in the hands of the police, they pushed through and triumphed. That phone call from the detective was the "Game Changer" in her relationship with her husband. It fortified her marriage and their relationship with their sons.

Monica Busanet

Monica Busanet is the wife of Cesar and the mother of two beautiful children Jaylyn and Aaliyah. She is a Human Resources Professional. She was born in Sumter, SC, and around age twelve, she moved with her family to the Pocono Mountains of Pennsylvania. After graduating from High School in Pennsylvania, she spent a year in a community college in New Jersey and joined the military shortly after. Monica spent eight years in the military deploying two times, once to Iraq and once to Afghanistan. After leaving the military, she obtained her Bachelor of Arts in Business Administration and her Master of Science in Leadership and Management, concentrating in Human Resource Management. She has always been passionate about writing, so when the opportunity to be a part of this book came along, she knew it would be right for her.

Shumon Spears Hudson

Shumon Hudson was born Shumon Spears in Charlotte, North Carolina. She is the oldest of two children and has been married for eight beautiful years. Through marriage, she has a blended family of five amazing young kings who created a blessed family. Spending time with family is essential for her.

She is a creative. She enjoys music, especially live bands and singing is her peace. She appreciates a good workout, quiet time doing yard work, and cooking when she has the time. People say she is good at it, and she agrees.

Shumon is grateful for every struggle that she has encountered in life as it has made her the woman she is today. It taught her to trust God and to believe in herself. She is grateful for peace in every area of her life, and she continues to strive for greatness in everything that she does.

Deleisha L Webb

Deleisha L. Webb lives in Charlotte, NC. She has a bachelor's degree in Family Studies and is a master's Level Social Worker. Deleisha currently works for Charlotte Mecklenburg Schools. She has over twenty years of experience in providing services to children and families. She is working on achieving her Licensure to become a Licensed Clinical Social Worker.

Deleisha is a divorced mother of one biological son and one bonus son. Both of her boys are grown and out of the house. Although she is an empty nester, her home is filled with noise and play as her sons have blessed her with two granddaughters, whom she loves, adores, and completely spoils.

Deleisha enjoys reading, writing, traveling, and spending time with her family.

Connect with Deleisha online:
Email: Deleishawebb@gmail.com
Facebook: https://www.facebook.com/deleisha.webbsmith
Instagram: https://www.instagram.com/deegirlwebb/

www.ingramcontent.com/pod-product-compliance
Lightning Source LLC
Chambersburg PA
CBHW071500080526
44587CB00014B/2162